Sold To Be A Wife

ONLY A DETERMINED FOSTER CARER CAN STOP A
TERRIFIED GIRL FROM BECOMING A CHILD BRIDE

MAGGIE HARTLEY

TRAPEZE

First published in 2018 by Trapeze,
an imprint of The Orion Publishing Group Ltd
Carmelite House, 50 Victoria Embankment,
London EC4Y 0DZ

An Hachette UK company

1 3 5 7 9 10 8 6 4 2

A CIP catalogue record for this book is
available from the British Library.

ISBN (Paperback): 978 1 409 17706 7
ISBN (eBook): 978 1 409 17707 4

Typeset by Born Group
Printed and bound in Great Britain by CPI Group UK

MIX
Paper from
responsible sources
FSC® C104740

www.orionbooks.co.uk

Dedication

This book is dedicated to Shazia, Michael and Louisa and all the children and teenagers who have passed through my home. It's been a privilege to have cared for you and to be able to share your stories. And to the children who live with me now. Thank you for your determination, strength and joy and for sharing your lives with me.

Contents

A Message from Maggie

I wanted to write this book to give people an honest account of what it's like to be a foster carer. To talk about some of the challenges that I face on a day-to-day basis and some of the children that I've helped.

My main concern throughout all this is to protect the children who have been in my care. For this reason all names and identifying details have been changed, including my own, and no locations have been included. But I can assure you that all my stories are based on real-life cases told from my own experiences.

Being a foster carer is a privilege and I couldn't imagine doing anything else. My house is never quiet but I wouldn't have it any other way. I hope perhaps my stories will inspire other people to consider fostering as new carers are always desperately needed.

Maggie Hartley

ONE

Truth and Lies

Squeezing the bottle over my head, I rubbed the oily liquid into my scalp.

'The joy of children,' I mumbled to myself as I made sure every strand of my shoulder-length brown hair was coated.

I'd just done a respite placement, looking after a six-year-old boy called Jake for a few days to give his permanent foster carer a break. Jake had gone now, but he'd kindly left me with a few little visitors to remind me of him.

Nits.

I'd felt the familiar tell-tale itch earlier that morning and sure enough, after a few moments of examining my scalp in the bathroom mirror, I'd found the evidence. I'd seen enough nits on children over the years to easily recognise them. So earlier today I'd rushed out to the chemist and bought a few bottles of expensive nit lotion and now I was smothering myself in it. Once I'd washed it out, I had my nit comb ready to give myself a thorough comb through.

1

My heart was already sinking at the thought of having to do the same thing on Michael, the wriggly 18-month-old I was fostering. I could barely keep him still long enough to change his nappy, never mind cover his gorgeous curls with nit lotion. He'd been with me for the past nine months since his mum Kerry had had a breakdown. After a spell in a psychiatric hospital, she was now thankfully back at home and the hope was that eventually Michael would be able to go back and live with her full time.

I knew the other occupant of my house wasn't going to be very happy about the nit situation either. Louisa was twenty, always immaculately made up and fashionably dressed, so she was going to be mortified at having to douse her glossy dark bob in nit shampoo. She'd lived with me since her parents had been killed in a car crash eight years ago and she was like my own daughter. She was out at work – she was a nanny for a local family – so I would have to break the bad news to her when she got home later.

While the lotion did its work, I decided to get on with some chores. I'd only just picked up the iron when my mobile rang.

'Maggie,' said a familiar voice. 'Can you talk?'

It was my supervising social worker Becky from the fostering agency that I worked for. We'd worked together for years now, so we knew each other well and she'd supported me through so many placements.

'Are you in the middle of something?' she asked.

'Only my ironing, so I'll gladly be disturbed,' I laughed. 'What can I do for you?'

'I wanted to see if you were available to help with an emergency placement,' she said. 'It's a fourteen-year-old girl

2

who Social Services have just got an EPO out on in the past hour. They need someone to take her for at least the weekend.'

An EPO is an emergency protection order designed to protect children whom Social Services felt were at immediate risk. It was Friday afternoon but there was always a judge on duty 24 hours a day who could issue one quickly. As was often the case with my placements, I knew I would have to make a quick decision based on little or no information. I was only fostering Michael at the moment and I had another spare bedroom.

'Yes of course,' I told her. 'I'd be happy to help out.'

'I'm afraid I don't know much about what's happening,' said Becky. 'All I know is that some sort of information has come to light while the girl has been at school today and Social Services don't feel it's safe for her to go home this weekend to her parents. She's still at school now and that's where the social worker wants you to go and collect her from. The social worker is called Rachel Myers, and she'll be able to fill you in on the specifics when you get up there.'

I grabbed a pen while Becky gave me the name and address of the school.

'That's about half an hour's drive from me,' I said. 'When do they want me to get her?'

'Ideally, as soon as possible,' said Becky. 'Are you OK to go now?'

I caught a glimpse of myself in the mirror and suddenly remembered the nit lotion. My hair looked like an oil slick.

'I can, but I'm afraid I look a bit of a state,' I told her.

Becky laughed as I explained about the nit lotion.

'Can't you quickly wash it out?' she asked.

'Becky, this stuff costs £10 a bottle,' I said. 'It's only been on for ten minutes and you have to leave it on at least an hour for it to work. I don't want to fork out for another lot.'

'Oh Maggie, you do make me chuckle,' she laughed. 'I'm sure nobody's going to care how you look.'

I knew she was right, but that didn't stop me from feeling slightly silly as I got into the car with my slicked-back greasy hair with its overpowering chemical smell. Michael wasn't due to be dropped off for another couple of hours so at least it gave me plenty of time to get up to the school and back.

As I drove, I thought about what Becky had told me. I had no idea what sort of situation I was about to face, and I was intrigued to know what had happened to this girl. A lot of carers shy away from fostering teens, but I had always enjoyed the challenge and I found them very interesting. It was also helpful having Louisa around when I was fostering a teenage girl as they tended to look up to her.

Eventually I pulled up into the car park of the school – a huge modern secondary on the other side of town. I had a quick glance at my greasy hair in the rearview mirror and then walked across the car park to the front entrance where there was an office behind a glass front. As I approached the hatch, a woman got up and came over to me.

'I'm Maggie Hartley,' I explained. 'I'm a foster carer here to see a Rachel Myers from Social Services.'

'Oh yes,' she said. 'They're expecting you. They're with Mrs White – she's the head teacher.'

I followed her down a corridor where she knocked on a door.

'Come in,' said a voice.

'This is Maggie Hartley, the foster carer,' she explained.

A woman in her early thirties was sat behind a desk. She looked very business-like in a trouser suit and shirt and she seemed young to be the head of such a large secondary school.

'I'm Anna White, the head here,' she smiled, shaking my hand.

I knew instantly the other woman must be the social worker. She had that slightly frazzled look that many social workers have and was dressed a lot more casually in black trousers and a grey waterfall cardigan. I could tell from the familiar colours of the lanyard she was wearing around her neck that she was from the local Social Services.

'Hi, I'm Rachel, Shazia's social worker,' she said, standing up and shaking my hand vigorously. 'Thanks so much for getting here so quickly.'

Shazia. At least I had a name now.

'No problem at all,' I said. 'I'm happy to help.'

'So Maggie, we'd better fill you in on what's been happening,' said Rachel.

'Yes, it's been quite a morning,' sighed Mrs White.

Rachel explained that Shazia was a Muslim and her parents were originally from Pakistan.

'This morning Shazia's best friend Zeena went to their form teacher and said that Shazia had locked herself in the toilet and was refusing to come out,' Mrs White explained.

'When Mrs Roebuck asked why, Zeena said it was because Shazia was scared as her parents were taking her to Pakistan this weekend and she was being forced into an arranged marriage with her cousin.'

Gosh, that hadn't been what I was expecting. I'd heard of forced marriages, of course, but naively I didn't think it was something that happened to young women living in our ordinary city.

'Zeena said Shazia didn't want to go to Pakistan, and when she told her parents that, her dad and one of her brothers beat her up,' Mrs White continued.

She went on to explain that after a lot of coaxing, the teacher had managed to persuade Shazia to come out of the toilet.

'She refused to answer mine or Mrs Roebuck's questions,' she said. 'In fact she wouldn't say anything. However, we did see bruises on her neck and face and that's when we decided to call Social Services.'

'Have you talked to Shazia?' I asked Rachel.

She nodded.

'Yes, although she's not saying much. She swears that she made the whole thing up and was only joking.'

'What about the bruises?' I asked.

'Reckons she accidentally walked into a kitchen cupboard,' shrugged Rachel. 'That might explain the bruising under her eye, but it wouldn't account for the marks on her neck. When I said we would have to call her parents to discuss what had happened, she became extremely panicky and upset and said they were going to go mad. She was begging me not to.'

Rachel explained that she had spoken to Zeena too.

'She's very concerned about her friend and she swears that Shazia's telling the truth about the forced marriage.'

At this point in time, forced marriage in the UK wasn't a crime, although the police could intervene. Marriages that take place overseas are not legally recognised in the UK.

'My manager spoke to the police a few hours ago and they've confirmed that three flights have been booked in Shazia and her parents' names to leave tonight for Pakistan,' continued Rachel. 'They were open tickets with no return and the school knew nothing about this.'

Mrs White shook her head.

'We therefore have to take this seriously,' said Rachel. 'We need to know Shazia is safe over the weekend while we look into the allegations a bit more.'

'Poor girl,' I sighed. 'She must be terrified.'

'She's still insisting that she made it all up,' said Mrs White, shaking her head.

It was horrendous to think that a fourteen-year-old girl could be taken to another country and forced to marry someone against her will. She was practically still a child.

'What have her parents said?' I asked.

'They've denied everything,' Rachel replied. 'They said they had an argument with Shazia this morning and that she's made up this story to get back at them.'

'But what about the bruises and the flights?' I asked.

'They said they didn't know anything about the bruises,' shrugged Rachel. 'They admitted that they were due to go to Pakistan this weekend for a family wedding and said they hadn't told the school as Shazia was only going to be off on Monday and Tuesday.

'They're absolutely furious at the idea of her being taken into care, particularly when I explained that I was unable to find a Muslim carer who would take her at such short notice.'

Wherever possible, children in care are placed with foster parents of the same ethnicity or religious beliefs.

'I did explain that it would be easier for them to work with me and that we could either take Shazia into care with their consent while we looked into things further or else we would apply for an EPO. They made it very clear they weren't willing to work with us, hence the EPO.'

'How's Shazia now?' I asked.

'Understandably very scared and very bewildered,' sighed Rachel. 'I'll take you through to see her now.'

'She's with Mrs Roebuck,' Mrs White added.

She led us down a long corridor and into a classroom. An older woman with curly blonde hair whom I assumed to be Mrs Roebuck sat at a desk at the front and gave us a nod of acknowledgement as we entered. At the back of the class, a girl was leant on a desk, her head in her hands. She looked up as we came in, staring at us with huge brown eyes. I could see the dark shadow of a bruise under one eye and on her cheekbone.

She had long dark hair tied back in a ponytail and despite the fact that it was a warm summer's day, she was wearing thick black leggings under her school skirt. She was very thin, and her arms and legs were like twigs.

'Who's this, Miss?' she asked Mrs White when she saw me. 'What's happening?'

She looked terrified.

'It's OK, Shazia,' Rachel reassured her. 'This is Maggie. She's the foster carer that I was telling you about. You're going to stay at her house for the weekend.'

'But I told you it wasn't true,' she cried, her huge eyes filling with tears. 'I was only joking and stupid Zeena believed me. I want to go home.'

'Shazia, we've already been through this,' Rachel told her gently. 'We can't let you go home until we know that you're safe. We have to take allegations of forced marriage very seriously and we can't risk that happening to you.'

'But I'm not marrying anyone,' she sighed. 'My parents are going to kill me. I was making it all up, I swear.'

I sat down on the desk next to her and gave her a reassuring smile.

'I know you must be scared,' I said. 'But all that's going to happen is that you'll come to my house this weekend while Social Services speak to your parents. Do you want me to tell you a bit about my house and who lives there?'

Shazia shrugged and although she didn't look too interested, I carried on.

'Do you like babies?' I asked her.

'Sometimes,' she shrugged.

'Well, there's Michael who's eighteen months old,' I told her. 'He's very cute, but he's always getting into mischief. He loves cars and is obsessed with his toy garage. Then there's Louisa. She's twenty and she works as a nanny.'

'Have you got a husband?' she asked.

'No,' I said. 'It's just me, Louisa and Michael.'

'You'll have your own bedroom,' I explained. 'It's a nice big room and there are bunk beds and a single bed in there so you can choose which one you want to sleep in.'

'But what will I wear?' she asked. 'I haven't got anything with me.'

'Well, on the way home we can stop at the supermarket and I'll get you a few toiletries and you can pick out some underwear and pyjamas and a few other bits and pieces,' I told her. 'Does that sound OK?'

Shazia nodded, although she still looked like a rabbit caught in the headlights.

'Don't worry, Shazia,' soothed Rachel. 'It's going to be OK. You're going to be fine with Maggie and I'll talk to you over the weekend and see how you're getting on.'

'Can I come back to school on Monday, Miss?' Shazia asked Mrs Roebuck anxiously.

She looked at Rachel for guidance.

'At this stage, I don't see why not,' Rachel nodded.

'We had better start heading back soon, lovey,' I told Shazia. 'Michael's mum will be dropping him home soon so I have to be there.'

Reluctantly, she picked up her rucksack.

'Maggie, I'll give you a ring later,' Rachel told me as we left.

As we walked out of the classroom, a girl came out of another door further down the corridor. When she saw us, she came running over.

'Shaz, where are you going?' she gasped.

'I've got to go to this lady's house for the weekend,' Shazia said glumly.

'But are you coming back?'

Shazia shrugged.

'Don't know. Think so.'

Mrs White came out behind us.

'Zeena, what are you doing here?' she asked. 'Go back to your classroom please.'

'I was just going to the loo, Miss, but then I saw Shaz and I wanted to say goodbye.'

Zeena turned to Shazia with tears in her eyes.

'I'm so sorry, Shaz,' she said. 'I only told because I didn't want you to go to Pakistan and I could see how scared you were.'

'It's OK,' Shazia sighed. 'They're going to sort it out.'

The girls gave each other a hug and Zeena went back into her classroom.

'Well Shazia, you take care over the weekend and all being well we'll see you on Monday,' Mrs White told her gently.

'OK, Miss,' she said.

'Thanks for your help,' I smiled at the head before we left.

Shazia was very quiet as we walked to the car.

'You're lucky to have a good friend like Zeena,' I said. 'She obviously cares about you a lot.'

Shazia smiled for the first time.

'Yeah, me and Zee have been besties since primary.'

She didn't say much for the rest of the journey so I chit-chatted away to her to try and break the ice.

'I'm sorry about my greasy hair,' I said. 'I had to put nit lotion on it earlier as a boy I was looking after earlier in the week gave me nits.'

'Yuck,' said Shazia, wrinkling her nose. 'That's gross.'

At least it gave us something to talk about.

There was just enough time to call into the local super-market before Michael was due back.

'Let's quickly sort you out with a few bits and pieces,' I said, pulling into the car park. 'We need to get you some clothes for the weekend.'

'What do you normally wear at home?' I asked.

'A shalwar kameez,' she said. 'You know, the long tunic top over trousers?'

'Yes, I know what you mean,' I said. I knew we weren't going to find it in Sainsbury's.

'You're probably only going to be with me for the weekend so let's see what we can get,' I told her. 'We can wash your school uniform and have it ready for Monday.'

'What about food?' I asked. 'Are you vegetarian?'

'No,' she said. 'But I only eat halal meat and no pork.'

I'd fostered children before who ate halal meat and I knew most of the supermarkets stocked it now. As a carer, I know that it's massively important to respect a child's religious beliefs and their customs.

'How about halal chicken and chips tonight and maybe pasta and a tomato sauce tomorrow?' I asked. 'Would you eat that?'

'Yeah,' she laughed. 'Course I'd eat that. My mum would never cook that at home, but I eat stuff like that at school all the time.'

At the supermarket we picked up some toiletries, a pair of slippers, knickers and pyjamas. The closest we could get to a shalwar kameez was a couple of pairs of leggings and two cotton tunic tops with long sleeves.

'Will these be OK for the weekend?' I asked.

'Yeah, I really like them,' she smiled, seeming pleased.

We drove back to the house and Shazia followed me nervously up the front path.

'Come on in and I'll show you where you'll be sleeping,' I told her gently as we walked into the hallway.

'Where's the baby and the other girl you were telling me about?' she asked anxiously, looking around.

'Michael's seeing his mum and she's going to drop him back here in a little while and Louisa's still at work,' I explained.

'She normally finishes a bit early on a Friday so you'll be able to meet them both later.'

I picked up the supermarket bags and she followed me upstairs to the spare bedroom. I really liked this room. It was light and bright and it overlooked the garden at the back of the house. It was painted a neutral cream colour and I'd cosied it up with a couple of lamps, a bright stripy rug and some pretty floral curtains that my friend Vicky had made.

'As I said, you can decide which bed you'd like to sleep in,' I told her. 'They've all got clean bedding on them.'

'That one,' she said, pointing to the top bunk. 'I've always wanted a high bed like that.'

She seemed quite excited at first, but as I put the things we'd bought from the supermarket into the chest of drawers, she sat down on the bed and suddenly looked like a frightened little girl.

'How long am I going to be here?' she asked, her big brown eyes full of worry.

I sat down on the bed next to her.

'I wish I could tell you but I don't honestly know, sweetie,' I said. 'Definitely the weekend though. On Monday Rachel's going to talk to your parents again and try to get to the bottom of what's been going on.'

'But why?' she frowned. 'Why does she have to talk to them? I've told you, I was making it all up. Why can't I just go home?'

'I'm afraid it's not as simple as that,' I told her. 'I know it's hard, but the school was worried enough about what you told Zeena to call Social Services. And it's Social Services' job to keep all children safe. So until we know that you're safe, we can't risk letting you go back home. OK?'

'But I am safe,' she sighed. 'I made it all up. That's the truth. Why won't anyone believe me?'

I could see she was upset but to be honest, I didn't know who or what to believe. She was saying one thing, her friend was saying another and her parents were denying everything. It was going to take a while to get to the bottom of this mess.

TWO

Settling In

Shazia looked as confused as I felt. As she wiped the tears from her eyes, I saw her wince as her hand touched the bruise on her cheekbone.

'That looks painful,' I said. 'I can get you some arnica cream to help it heal if you'd like?'

'No, I'm alright,' she replied, looking at the floor. 'I just walked into a kitchen cupboard, that's all.'

'What about those marks on your neck?' I asked.

I could just see the top of a blue bruise poking out above the collar of her white school shirt.

'No, it's fine,' she snapped, covering the bruise with her hand. 'When I walked into the cabinet door the metal handle thingy jabbed me in my throat.'

She didn't sound very convincing, but I didn't challenge her or push her any further. She'd had a hard day and she looked exhausted.

'Michael will be back soon so I'd better go and get this nit lotion washed off,' I told her.

'I'll leave you to get settled in. Feel free to have a wander downstairs if you like. The telly's in the front room. I'll show you around properly once I've got this stuff off,' I continued, gesturing at my hair.

'OK,' she said, giving me a weak smile. 'Thanks.'

I spent the next twenty minutes in the shower desperately trying to scrub out the oily lotion. As I shampooed my hair for the fourth time, I thought about Shazia. My first impressions of her were that she seemed like a sweet girl. She wasn't bolshie and she didn't have lots of attitude like many of the teens who had come into my care over the years. She seemed very polite and respectful.

After my shower, I went back downstairs where I found Shazia watching MTV in the front room.

'Are you OK, lovey?' I asked her.

'Yeah, fine,' she mumbled, engrossed in the television.

'I'm not normally allowed to watch stuff like this at home,' she told me, looking up from the screen. 'I'm not really allowed to watch any TV at all.'

'Really?' I said, not managing to disguise my surprise.

She was watching ordinary music videos that I would have thought were normal viewing for most teenagers.

'I'm sorry,' I told her. 'I didn't realise.'

'Don't worry,' she smiled. 'I like it.'

Rachel hadn't said anything to me about stopping her from watching TV, but I made a mental note to mention it to her the next time I saw her. I needed to cover my own back and also to get her advice on whether I should let her if her parents didn't allow it at home.

I was on my way to the kitchen to get Shazia a drink and snack when the doorbell rang.

It was Kerry dropping Michael back.

'Come in,' I told her, grinning at them both.

'Hello gorgeous,' I cooed as I saw Michael wriggling around in her arms. 'Have you had a lovely time with Mummy?'

He looked like a little cherub with his long spidery eyelashes and dark curls. He gave me a big grin and as soon as Kerry put him down on the floor, he toddled off.

'How did you get on?' I asked her.

It was only the second time that she'd had unsupervised contact at her flat.

'It was brilliant to have him on his own,' she said happily. 'We did some painting and he watched a bit of Peppa Pig.'

'Oh yes, he loves his Peppa,' I smiled. 'Good. I'm really pleased.'

Kerry was in her early twenties and she was a tiny slip of a woman. She was very pale and thin and her eyes had that glazed look of someone who was on a lot of medication.

'How are you doing?' I asked her. 'You look tired.'

'I'm OK,' she shrugged. 'These new tablets I'm on are playing havoc with my sleep so I'm trying to get used to them. But I am feeling a lot stronger.'

'Well, like your counsellor said, it's going to take time,' I told her. 'You're doing so well.'

'I just want my baby back now, Maggie,' she sighed.

'I know you do,' I said, giving her a sympathetic smile.

Just then I noticed Michael had gone into the living room where Shazia was watching TV.

'Come through and I'll introduce you to the young lady who's staying with us this weekend,' I told Kerry.

Michael was sat next to Shazia on the sofa and she was showing him the remote control.

'Shazia, I can see you've already met Michael,' I smiled at her. 'And this is his mum Kerry.'

'He's really cute,' Shazia grinned.

'Don't be fooled,' Kerry told her. 'He is very cute, but he can be a right little monkey when he wants to, can't he, Maggie?'

'He can,' I laughed. 'You need eyes in the back of your head.'

After we'd swapped pleasantries, Kerry said goodbye to Michael and left to catch the bus back home while I got on with cooking dinner, leaving Shazia to watch TV in peace.

Tea was almost ready when I heard Louisa's key in the front door. I went out to meet her in the hallway.

'Thank God it's Friday,' she sighed as she put down her bag. 'Ooh, something smells nice,' she said, sniffing the air.

'Chicken and chips,' I told her. 'It will be ready in five minutes. But before we eat, there's someone I'd like to introduce you to.'

Louisa looked surprised as Shazia wandered out into the hallway from the living room.

'Louisa, this is Shazia and she's going to be staying with us for a couple of days.'

'Hi Shazia,' smiled Louisa.

'I really like your shoes,' Shazia said shyly, as Louisa took off her Vans trainers.

'Thanks,' she replied. 'Maggie got me them for my birthday.'

While the girls set the table, I strapped Michael into his highchair and served up dinner.

'Sorry it's so noisy, Shazia,' I laughed as Michael banged his beaker on the tray of his highchair. 'Does your family normally eat together when you're at home?'

'No, I eat at a table in the kitchen and my brothers and my dad eat in a different room,' Shazia replied.

'Oh, so you never eat all together?' Louisa asked, surprised. Shazia shook her head.

'What about your mum?' I asked.

'She sits with me in the kitchen,' she told us. 'In our house the women always eat separately to the men.'

'But what about if you have people round?' Louisa pressed on, clearly fascinated.

'If my aunties and uncles come round, it's the same,' Shazia explained. 'My aunties sit with us and my uncles go and sit with my dad and brothers.'

'So you never, ever sit together?' asked Louisa.

Shazia shook her head and I noticed her cheeks flushing red.

'Gosh, isn't it interesting how different cultures all have different traditions?' I said quickly. 'It's fascinating hearing how other families do things.'

I got up to pick up Michael's plate that he had thrown on the floor. As I sat back down, I put my hand on Louisa's shoulder to signal to her to leave it there.

I was conscious of us asking Shazia too many questions about her home life. I didn't want her to feel bombarded.

'How's your chicken, Shazia?' I asked, trying to change the subject.

'Lovely, thank you,' she replied.

As soon as we'd all finished, Shazia jumped up and started collecting the empty plates together.

'I can wash up,' she said.

'It's OK, I got a dishwasher a few months ago,' I told her. 'I don't think I could be without it now.'

'Well, I'll scrape the plates and rinse them then,' she said eagerly.

'Thank you,' I told her, surprised. 'That's really helpful.'

After dinner, Louisa and Shazia watched TV while I got Michael bathed and ready for bed. When I came back downstairs, I could tell Shazia was exhausted.

'Why don't you go up now too, lovey?' I suggested. 'You've had a long day and you must be shattered.'

'I am a bit,' she admitted.

'I'll come up in ten minutes and say goodnight,' I told her.

Louisa made me a cup of tea and we sat in the front room.

'Are you allowed to tell me why Shazia's here?' she asked in a low voice.

I would never share private information with another child, but as Louisa was an adult and not in the care system, I felt it was only fair to tell her the truth. I knew she would keep the information confidential.

'Social Services are worried that her parents were going to take her to Pakistan and force her into an arranged marriage,' I explained.

Louisa looked shocked.

'But she's only a young girl,' she gasped. 'That's awful.'

I nodded.

'They're still looking into the allegations but that's what Shazia told her friend.'

'I read about that happening to someone in a magazine once, but I didn't think it was something that happened to ordinary girls,' replied Louisa.

'In a way, I hope she has made it all up as I wouldn't wish it on anyone,' I sighed. 'Obviously please keep this information to yourself and don't ask Shazia about it,' I added.

'Oh no, you know I'd never say anything, Maggie, I promise.'

I knew she wouldn't.

When I went upstairs, Shazia was sat on the single bed in her pyjamas.

'How are you doing?' I asked her.

She looked up at me, her dark eyes filled with tears.

'I miss my mum,' she cried. 'I want to go home.'

'I know you do, lovey, but remember you're going to stay here with me for the weekend and then on Monday, after Rachel's spoken with your mum and dad, she'll talk to you again and hopefully things will be a lot clearer,' I told her.

'Whatever happens, you'll definitely be able to see your parents on Monday. Rachel said she was going to sort that out.'

'They're going to be so angry with me,' Shazia sobbed.

I wasn't sure whether she meant they'd be cross with her for making things up or because she'd told the truth.

'Listen, all families have their ups and downs,' I soothed. 'I'm sure your parents are missing you just as much as you're missing them. Whatever's happened you'll find a way through it.'

I could see how upset Shazia was.

'Try and get some sleep,' I told her kindly. 'It's been a horrible day for you, but things will seem better in the morning. OK?'

She gave me a tearful smile.

'Night night,' I told her. 'Call me if you need anything.'

I was shattered too and it wasn't long before I was in bed as well. I hadn't heard a word from Shazia and when I peeped around her door on the way back from the bathroom, I was relieved to see that she was fast asleep on the top bunk.

Michael woke up at seven as usual, but both Louisa and Shazia were still fast asleep. Shazia still wasn't awake when Rachel called at nine.

'Morning, Maggie,' she said breezily. 'I just wanted to give you a quick call to see how Shazia is.'

'She's still in bed at the moment,' I told her.

'Typical teenager,' she laughed. 'How's she been?'

'She's fine,' I said. 'There were a few tears last night as she's a bit overwhelmed by everything, understandably, but overall she's been OK. She seems like a really sweet girl.'

'What are your plans for the weekend?' Rachel asked.

'To be honest, probably not a lot,' I told her. 'I'm going to keep things very low key. We might go for a walk later.'

'Good idea,' she replied.

'What should I do if Shazia asks to go out on her own or meet friends?' I asked.

She was fourteen and I couldn't really keep her in.

'That should be OK,' she reassured me. 'Her family live quite a way from you in a different area and they don't know your address. If she does ask, though, I'd keep it to a couple of hours and make sure she stays local,' Rachel suggested. 'Get her to go somewhere near you rather than going into the centre of town.'

'OK,' I said. 'She might not even ask but it's best to be prepared.'

By the time Shazia woke up at 10 o'clock, Louisa had already gone to her boyfriend Charlie's house.

Shazia was very quiet and sleepy.

'Do you want some breakfast?' I asked her.

'No thanks,' she said. 'Is it OK if I use the bathroom?'

'Yes of course,' I replied. 'There are some fresh towels in your bedroom.'

Shazia was in there for absolutely ages. I heard the shower stop after ten minutes, but she was still in there half an hour later.

'Are you OK in there?' I asked, concerned.

'Yeah, fine,' she called.

When she was finally dressed and ready, I suggested that we all went for a walk in the woods.

'I think the fresh air would do us good,' I said.

A lot of teenagers would have huffed and puffed and kicked up a fuss about going for a walk but Shazia was very compliant.

'I just need the loo,' she said, so I got Michael into his buggy while she went to the toilet.

I was stood there for a good twenty minutes before she reappeared again.

'Are you OK, Shazia?' I asked her. 'Have you got a tummy ache?'

'No, no, I'm fine,' she said quickly.

It was odd that she spent so much time in the toilet and it was another thing to mention to Rachel.

We had a good tramp through the local woods. Shazia didn't say much, but she chased around after Michael and seemed OK.

'Can I ring my friend Zeena?' Shazia asked after we'd come home and had lunch.

'Yes, of course you can,' I told her, surprised. 'Do you have your own mobile?'

She shook her head.

'No, I'm not allowed one,' she said.

I picked up the landline.

'Tell me the number and I'll type it in for you,' I asked her.

I made sure I put '141' in front of it so my phone number wouldn't show up on her friend's phone. As a foster carer, I always have to be careful about who has my number for security reasons so I try to avoid giving it out. If children do give out my address or phone number, often they don't realise it's not just themselves they're putting in jeopardy, it's the other children I have living with me too.

'I'm going to put you on speakerphone because I need to know who you're talking to,' I told her.

'But I told you I was ringing Zeena,' she complained.

'I just need to check that, sweetie, I'm afraid,' I said. 'It's not that I don't trust you, I just can't take the risk.'

'OK,' she sighed.

I could see she felt a bit awkward having me listening as Zeena answered.

'Zee, it's me,' she said.

'Shaz, are you OK?' Zeena replied anxiously. 'Are you still at that lady's house?'

'Yeah, I'm still here,' she mumbled, obviously feeling self-conscious that I was listening in.

It was clearly her mate Zeena that she was talking to, so after a few minutes I let her take it off speakerphone although I made sure I hovered around while they were chatting.

'Yeah, Zee,' I heard her say. 'I would, but I'll have to ask OK?'

24

She put the phone down and came out to the kitchen where I was loading the dishwasher.

'Would I be allowed to go and meet Zeena?' she asked me hesitantly.

'This is a foster home not a prison, lovey,' I smiled. 'That should be fine. I'd like you to stay nearby though. Maybe you could go and have a look round the local village? Do you think that will be OK with Zeena?'

'Should be,' she said. 'Her mum can drop her off.'

She called Zeena back and I told her which bus to catch. The bus stop was practically outside the house and it only took five minutes to the centre of the village.

'I've got a spare pay-as-you-go mobile here that I you can take with you,' I told her. 'Then we can ring each other if needs be.'

It was useful to have to give to teenagers that I was fostering when they went out. Also, because it belonged to me, I could check who they were texting or ringing and also see who was messaging them.

'Have a good time,' I told her. 'Give me a ring if there are any problems and remember to be back for four o'clock.'

'I will,' she said.

Even though she was only getting the bus to the village ten minutes down the road and Rachel had given permission for her to go out, I was still on tenterhooks while she was gone. I always felt anxious when a new placement went out as I didn't really know her friendship group and I hadn't known her long enough to sense if she was trustworthy.

Michael was having a nap so I spent the next couple of hours cleaning to try and distract myself from worrying.

When 4 p.m. came and there was no sign of Shazia, I had a sick feeling gnawing away in my stomach. I picked up the phone and rang the mobile. It rang and rang but there was no answer. Finally it clicked onto voicemail.

'Shazia, it's Maggie,' I said. 'It's four o'clock – where are you? I need you to head back now. Please can you ring me to let me know you're on the way and if you're stuck I can come and collect you.'

When it got to half past four, I knew I needed to ring it in to my fostering agency. I explained what had happened to a duty social worker.

'Her social worker agreed it was OK but she's half an hour late,' I told her. 'She has a mobile with her but she's not answering it. I'm hoping she sees my missed call.'

'OK, let's not panic just yet,' the duty social worker reassured me. 'Give her another half an hour and if she still isn't back, you'll need to phone it in to the local authority.'

I felt really annoyed at myself for letting her go out. I should have just said no when she asked as it wasn't worth the risk. All I could hope was that she was safe and she hadn't done anything silly like try and contact her family or go back home to her parents.

Suddenly I had visions of her being bundled into a car and driven at high speed to the airport. At this very moment she could be getting on a plane bound for Pakistan and it would be too late to stop her. I felt sick to my stomach. What had I done?

THREE

Contact and Conflict

Pacing up and down the living room, I had one eye on the clock and another on the front window.

'Come on, Shazia, where are you?' I thought to myself.

Even Michael was looking up at me strangely, as if he could sense my anguish as he played with his toys on the floor.

I couldn't get the image of Shazia being bundled onto a plane to Pakistan out of my mind and my stomach was churning with dread.

By 4.50 I was feeling frantic and was about to ring in to Social Services when suddenly there was a knock at the door.

I rushed to open it, only to find a happy-looking Shazia standing on the doorstep.

'Hi Maggie,' she smiled breezily, like she didn't have a care in the world.

'Where on earth have you been?' I exclaimed. 'I was worried sick.'

'I was in the village with Zeena like you said,' she replied, looking confused.

'You were supposed to be back at four,' I told her, exasperated. 'You're nearly an hour late. I've been ringing and ringing the mobile but you never answered.'

'Oh were you?' she said, surprised. 'I didn't see the time and I never heard the phone.'

She rummaged in her pocket for it.

'I think it's on silent,' she said as she fished it out and examined the screen. 'I'm really sorry, I didn't realise.'

'It's OK,' I sighed, relief flooding through my body. 'I'm just glad you're alright. You had me worried there. I was about to call Social Services.'

Perhaps I had overreacted and I tried to banish all thoughts of planes to Pakistan out of my mind once and for all.

'Anyway, did you have a good time?' I asked.

Shazia nodded happily.

'It was sick,' she grinned. 'Me and Zee had a look in some shops and then we went to a café for a hot chocolate.'

'That sounds nice,' I said. 'Is that the kind of thing you normally do when you meet up with your friends?'

'I've never been allowed to do it before,' she said. 'My parents don't like me going out on my own.'

'Oh,' I said, surprised.

I didn't say anything but inside I wondered if I had done the wrong thing in letting her go out, even though Rachel had given her permission.

From what she'd told me so far, quite a lot of restrictions had been placed on Shazia. She couldn't watch TV, have a mobile phone or go out with friends. These were all things that I considered as 'normal' activities for a fourteen-year-old. I had to respect the fact that Shazia came from a different culture to mine, though, and it was definitely something I needed to talk to Rachel about. It was clear to me that, perhaps because of her sheltered upbringing, Shazia was very naïve and I would think twice about letting her go out independently again.

Thankfully the rest of the weekend passed quietly without incident. Louisa was staying at Charlie's for the weekend, and I sensed that Shazia was disappointed not to be able to spend more time with her.

On Monday morning, Shazia was already up by the time I came downstairs with Michael just before seven.

'You're up early,' I said.

'I couldn't sleep,' she sighed.

I could tell that the thought of seeing her parents again was preying on her mind.

'Are you worried about seeing your mum and dad?' I asked her gently.

She nodded.

'I know they're going to go mad at me,' she mumbled, fiddling with the hem of her pyjama top.

'It probably won't be as bad as you think,' I reassured her. 'I bet they'll be so pleased to see you.'

'What's going to happen today?' she asked suddenly, her big brown eyes wide. 'After I've seen them, will I go home with them?'

'Shazia, I know you're not going to like my answer,' I sighed. 'But like I've been telling you all weekend, I honestly don't know, lovey. Rachel will be talking to you and your parents again today and hopefully everything will be sorted out soon. Whatever happens, you know you'll definitely be seeing them later.'

There was a part of me that thought by the end of the day she might actually be allowed to go home, so I fished out a spare rucksack from the cupboard under the stairs.

'Why don't you pack your things in this bag just in case, and then if you do end up going home I can drop this straight to Rachel,' I told her.

I could tell that Shazia was torn about the thought of contact. She was obviously missing her parents and wanted to see them, but unsurprisingly she was clearly worried about their reaction to her revelations at school.

'Maggie, you know when I see my parents later, will you come with me?' she asked, looking up at me pleadingly.

'If you want me there, then of course I'm happy to come along,' I told her. 'But I'll have to check that it's OK with Rachel first and even if I am there, it would just be for moral support. I wouldn't be allowed to intervene,' I warned her. 'I'd be there as an observer.'

'That's fine,' she nodded, looking relieved.

I made her some toast but she just picked at it.

'Why don't you go upstairs and sort your things out and get into your school uniform,' I told her. 'I'll finish feeding Michael his porridge and get him ready.'

An hour later we all got into the car and I dropped her off outside the school.

'Have a good day,' I smiled at her. 'I'll be here at half past three to pick you up and take you straight to contact.'

'Will you talk to the social worker lady today?' she asked.

'Yes,' I reassured her. 'Rachel's going to ring me this morning.'

On a Monday I normally took Michael to a rhyme time session at the local library, but I wasn't sure when Rachel was going to call and I didn't want to miss her.

It was after eleven when she rang.

'Morning, Maggie,' she said, 'How did the weekend go? How's Shazia been?'

'She's been OK,' I replied. 'There are a few bits and pieces I wanted to mention to you though.'

I told her about the things Shazia had said she wasn't normally allowed to do at home.

'They're all things that I'd deem as normal for most teenagers, but if she's not allowed to them at home, should I have been stopping her too?' I asked. 'I suppose I want to cover my back and let you know and also get your advice on it.'

'OK,' she said. 'That's all good to know. Let's see what happens today and if Shazia is with you a little bit longer then I'll talk to her parents and take a view on how we want to play it.'

There was one other thing I wanted to mention to Rachel.

'This is going to sound really strange but I've noticed that she spends an awfully long time in the toilet. I asked her if she had a stomach ache or anything but she insisted that she was fine.'

'I'll ask her parents to see if there have been any past medical problems or conditions that we need to know about,' Rachel reassured me.

Rachel updated me on where things were at with the case.

'I've been round to see Shazia's parents this morning and I've talked to Shazia at school.'

'What are you thinking?' I asked her.

'To be honest, Maggie, I'm none the wiser,' she sighed. 'Her parents are insisting that Shazia made the whole thing up, but something's still not sitting right with me. Why would she make up the fact that she was being forced into an arranged marriage and face getting into trouble with her parents? Why were those flights booked to Pakistan? Were they really for a family wedding?

'I don't feel like I really have a true picture of what's going on at all,' she added. 'So I'm going to wait and see how contact goes this afternoon and then talk to my manager about how best to proceed. Could you pick her up from school and have her at the contact centre for four o'clock, Maggie?'

'Shazia's asked if I could come along with her for moral support,' I told her. 'Is that OK with you?'

'Yes, she mentioned that to me this morning,' said Rachel. 'And I told her it was fine. In a way it might be a good idea for her parents to meet you. It might help put their minds at rest about where Shazia is staying as I know they were very concerned.'

'OK,' I said. 'Well in that case I'll see you later then.'

My mind kept drifting to Shazia as the day went on and I hoped she was OK. I knew how anxious she was about contact this morning and to be honest, I could empathise with how she was feeling. As a foster carer, you're always apprehensive about meeting any child's birth parents, but from what Rachel had told me, it seemed as though Shazia's parents were quite hostile and angry about the situation and I suspected they might not necessarily give me the warmest of welcomes.

★

That afternoon I got ready to take Shazia to see her parents. I'd dropped Michael off at Kerry's for their contact session earlier that afternoon, which was perfect timing as it meant that I didn't have to bring him along with me.

It was a warm June afternoon but something made me change out of the summer dress that I was wearing and put on some navy trousers and a long-sleeved cotton blouse. If I was meeting Shazia's parents, I wanted to be as respectful of their culture as I could and I was worried that I would feel uncomfortable having my bare arms and legs showing. I wanted things to go as smoothly as possible and I didn't want anyone to be distracted by my clothing or lack of it.

As I waited in the school car park for Shazia, I was surprised to see her walking towards me wearing the leggings and the blouse I'd bought her and not her school uniform.

'Hi,' I said to her. 'Have you had a good day?'

'It was OK,' she shrugged, getting into the front passenger seat.

'How come you're not wearing your uniform?' I asked.

'I felt really hot so I wanted to get changed after school,' she said.

'Are your parents going to be OK seeing you dressed like that or is it going to upset them?' I asked.

Shazia shrugged.

'I know it's not a shalwar kameez but my arms and legs are covered.'

I wasn't convinced and I hoped it wouldn't cause any issues with her mum and dad.

'The social worker lady came to see me at school today,' Shazia said, changing the subject.

'And what did she say?' I asked.

'She said the same as you,' she replied. 'She didn't know if I would be allowed to go home either, but she said she would have another chat with me after I'd seen my parents.'

'That sounds like a good plan,' I told her. 'I know it's hard not knowing what's happening, but everyone has got to be 100 per cent sure that you're safe.'

'I know,' she sighed. 'But I am safe. I keep telling you all that I made it up. Why won't anyone believe me?'

Shazia fell silent as we got closer to the contact centre and I could feel her physically tense up as we pulled into the car park.

'Don't worry,' I reassured her. 'It will be OK.'

As we got out of the car and walked towards the front entrance, I noticed an Asian lad in his twenties having a cigarette outside the building.

'Oh, that's my brother Adil,' gasped Shazia, a worried look on her face. 'He must have driven my mum and dad here.'

He looked very Western in his designer jeans, trainers and leather jacket. As soon as he saw us, he came marching over.

'What the hell are you wearing, Shaz?' he asked her, grabbing at her arm.

'Get off me, Adil,' she snapped. 'Leave me alone. You can't tell me what to do.'

'Come on, otherwise we're going to be late,' I said hurriedly, steering Shazia in front of me so her brother couldn't get to her.

I was shocked by his behaviour but I didn't say anything as I wanted to avoid a confrontation and get Shazia inside as quickly as possible.

Adil shook his head, glaring at us, and stubbed out his cigarette.

As we walked into the reception, Rachel was there to meet us.

'Hi Shazia, your parents are already here and are waiting for you in the contact room,' she said.

Shazia looked nervous.

'Can Maggie come in with me?'

'Yes of course, that's fine,' smiled Rachel.

'Before we go in, can I have a quick word?' I asked Rachel quietly, and we went over the other side of the room where we were out of Shazia's earshot.

'Just to let you know, we ran into Shazia's brother in the car park outside,' I told her. 'He wasn't very happy with what she's wearing. She'd changed by the time I'd picked her up from school so I hope it's not going to cause any problems.'

'Well, even if it does there's not a lot we can do about it now,' sighed Rachel. 'Shazia's parents have asked if Adil can come into the contact session. I did say that was fine, but if there's any trouble I will ask him to leave.'

We went back over to where Shazia was waiting.

'Right then, let's go in,' said Rachel.

As she led us down a corridor I took a deep breath, unsure of the sort of reception we were about to face. We walked into the room to see a couple in their late fifties. Shazia's father had grey hair and was dressed traditionally in flowing beige trousers and a long top with buttons down the front. Her mum was dressed in a blue shalwar kameez and was wearing a hijab.

'Mr and Mrs Bains, this is Maggie Hartley,' Rachel began, introducing me to the couple.

'Oh, so you're the foster lady,' Shazia's father said, looking me up and down dismissively.

'Yes,' I smiled. 'Shazia has been staying with me this weekend. It's nice to meet you.'

I held out my hand to him and he shook it.

Shazia didn't say anything to her dad but went straight over to her mum. She crouched down on the floor and put her hands in her lap.

'I'm sorry, Mamma,' she sighed. 'I'm so sorry.'

Just then Shazia's brother came into the room and started having a conversation with his dad in Punjabi. It was obviously about Shazia as he kept pointing at her and I could tell by the tone of his voice that he was angry about something. I didn't have a clue what they were saying and I looked over at Rachel.

'Is there a problem, Mr Bains?' she asked.

He turned round to his son and put his hand on his arm as if to silence him.

'No, no, there's no problem,' he said quickly. 'My son was just saying how upsetting it is to see Shazia in those strange clothes.'

'Well you're very welcome to provide some clothes for Shazia if you're not happy,' she told him. 'I know that when Shazia went to stay with Maggie, all she had was her school uniform so they had to get what they could on Friday night to tide her over the weekend.'

Shazia was still crouched down beside her mum who was now talking to her in Punjabi. She sounded angry and it was clear she was giving her a real dressing down. Shazia burst into tears.

'I'm sorry,' she sobbed. 'I told them I made it all up, Mamma. I'm sorry for telling lies.'

He father raised his hand.

'That's enough, Shazia,' he said firmly. 'Stop talking now. You've brought enough shame on our family.'

At once Shazia dried her tears and sat down obediently.

Her father carried on talking to her, this time in Punjabi, and soon she was sobbing again.

I caught Rachel's eye and the expression on her face said it all. We both knew that she should have organised a translator for the session.

The contact session was in part an opportunity for Shazia to see her parents, but it was just as important for Rachel to see Shazia and her parents together and see how they interacted with each other. To do that fully, she needed to understand what they were saying.

'Mr Bains,' she said hurriedly, interrupting his rant. 'Please could I kindly request that you conduct your conversation in English.'

'I'm talking to my daughter and I'll talk to my daughter in whatever language I choose,' he replied angrily.

'I understand that, Mr Bains, and I respect your language, but I need to know what's being said,' she told him firmly. 'If you're not willing to speak in English, then I'm afraid I'll need to cut this contact session short.'

'You're saying I can't talk to my own child in my own language?' he snapped.

'No, I'm not saying that,' she replied calmly. 'Of course I'm happy for you to talk to your daughter, but as she's getting distressed I need to understand what you're saying to her. Your daughter's welfare and safety is my responsibility and if I don't know what's been said to her, I can't get a true picture of what's happening here. I apologise for not organising a translator for this session, but as you and your wife spoke very good English when I came to see you, I didn't think there was any need.'

'My daughter's distressed because she has told so many lies,' Mr Bains shot back.

He carried on ranting and raving at Shazia in Punjabi and before long, her brother Adil joined in. Shazia buried her head in her hands, her whole body wracked with sobs.

Rachel suddenly stood up.

'That's enough,' she said, raising her voice. 'I'm afraid I need to end this contact session now, Mr and Mrs Bains. Next time I will make sure that we have an interpreter on hand so you can talk to your daughter in whatever language you wish.

'Maggie, I think it's best that you and Shazia go now. I'll come and see you later,' she told me firmly.

I nodded.

'Come on, Shazia,' I said. 'We need to leave.'

I got up to go and Shazia hurriedly followed me out of the room, still sobbing. As she left, Shazia's mum gave her a weak smile while her dad and Adil were having what looked like a heated discussion in Punjabi.

And just like that, the first contact session came to a very abrupt end.

FOUR

A Niggling Feeling

As we left the contact room, Shazia looked as shell-shocked as I felt.

'Are you OK, Shazia?' I asked her, concerned. 'It sounded like you were getting a bit of a tongue-lashing in there.'

'My dad's just worried about me,' she replied shakily, drying her eyes on the hem of her blouse. 'He's angry because he thinks I've brought shame on the family and he's concerned about where I'm living.'

'I'm really sorry it ended so abruptly,' I sighed. 'Rachel needs to be able to hear what's been said between you and your parents, and as they were speaking in Punjabi, she wasn't able to do that.'

'They can speak good English, you know,' Shazia told me. 'I talk to them in English all the time.'

'Well, for whatever reason, they weren't willing to do that today,' I replied. 'And that's fine. As your father said, he can talk to you in whatever language he chooses. Next time, though, Rachel will organise an interpreter so if they want to talk to you in Punjabi she can still understand what's being said.'

I wanted to try and get Shazia out of the contact centre as quickly as possible. Emotions were running high and I was keen to avoid any possible confrontation between her and her brother or parents.

'Let's head back to the car,' I said, motioning towards the exit.

'But where am I going now?' she asked, her dark eyes wide. 'Can't I go home with them now?'

She looked so confused and my heart went out to her.

'I'm sorry, lovey, I don't think that's going to happen today,' I told her gently. 'I think it's going to be a few more days before Rachel and her managers can make that kind of a decision. She probably wants to wait and see how the next contact session goes.'

'But you said. . .'

'I said that I didn't know,' I explained, patiently. 'I know it's all really confusing for you right now, but Rachel will come and talk to you later.'

I could see she was upset, but all I could do was be honest with her and tell her the truth.

As we drove home, I tried to make conversation with her about her family.

'Your brother gave you a bit of a hard time,' I said. 'Do you get on well with your brothers?'

'Not really, they're always bossing me around and telling me what to do. Just like my dad.'

'What about your mum?' I asked her.

Shazia hesitated, tears pricking her eyes.

'I really miss my mum, Maggie,' she whispered, her voice cracking.

As soon as we got back to the house, Shazia went straight up to her room. I left her in peace as I thought she could probably do with some quiet time on her own to process the events of the afternoon.

Half an hour later, a harassed-looking Rachel came round.

'Well, that didn't go as I'd planned,' she sighed, flopping down at the kitchen table as I put the kettle on. 'I completely hold my hands up, it was all my fault. When I went to see Shazia's parents, they both spoke to me in perfect English so I naively assumed that at contact they would speak to each other in English and I didn't need to book an interpreter,' she continued. 'But I've learnt my lesson and I've apologised to them for that oversight.'

'We all make mistakes,' I told her. 'It can't be helped. Shazia was getting upset and you needed to know why. They could have worked with you and talked to each other in English, but they refused.'

'I need to explain things to Shazia too,' she sighed.

I called Shazia and she came downstairs. Her eyes were red and puffy and I could tell that she had been crying again. When she saw Rachel sitting in the kitchen, she instantly looked wary.

'I'm sorry we had to cut the contact session short today, Shazia,' Rachel told her once Shazia had sat down at the table. 'It's really important during contact that I know what's going on and what your parents are saying to you and vice versa. The situation seemed to be getting very heated and you were obviously getting upset.'

'Oh, it was nothing,' said Shazia quickly. 'It was all fine. My dad was just worried about me, that's all.'

'It's alright you telling me that, but I need to hear it for myself,' Rachel replied. 'So I've organised for you to have another contact session in a couple of days and this time I've arranged for one of our contact workers who speaks Punjabi to sit in on it.'

'Two days!' Shazia exclaimed, looking crestfallen. 'So I'm not going home now?'

'Not before the next contact session I'm afraid, no,' said Rachel gently.

'It's not fair,' Shazia yelled, her eyes filling with tears. 'I just want to go home.'

She stormed out, slamming the kitchen door behind her.

'She's just disappointed,' I told Rachel sympathetically.

'I know,' she replied. 'But something's still not sitting right with me. Her parents were really giving her a hard time about something today.'

'Well, if she did make up the story about them taking her to Pakistan for a forced marriage, I'm not surprised they were cross,' I said.

'I just feel uneasy,' Rachel told me, her brow furrowed. 'I get the feeling there's more going on than meets the eye, but I suppose we'll have to see. Shazia's parents were also very insistent that she should be wearing her own clothes whilst she's staying with you, so they're going to drop a bag of things into the office tomorrow. As soon as I get them, I'll bring them round to you,' she said.

'What about the other things I mentioned this morning?' I asked her. 'Should I still be letting her watch TV, and what should I say if she asks to go and meet her friends again?'

'Let me talk to her parents and then I'll take a view,' replied Rachel.

When Rachel left, I thought about all the children I'd fostered over the years from different cultures. It was so important that I respected their beliefs; otherwise it looked like I was devaluing them.

Sometimes, though, it could be a steep learning curve. The time that stood out most in my memory was the three young sisters I fostered a few years earlier who were Jehovah's Witnesses. I knew and accepted that if they ever needed to be taken into hospital they couldn't have blood transfusions, but I struggled with the fact that they weren't allowed Christmas presents. I got into a battle with Social Services because whilst I understood their religious beliefs, it felt cruel not to buy them presents when all the other children who lived with me were getting them. The compromise that we came to in the end was I didn't wrap their gifts up and I gave them to the girls a week before Christmas so technically they weren't associated with Christmas Day. It felt wrong to me that they wouldn't have new toys to play with and it felt like I would be leaving them out.

Language could often be tricky too. In the past I'd fostered children who didn't speak a word of English. Now, at least, there are translator apps you can download on your phone, but years ago I'd have to type sentences into my computer to try and translate what I needed to say, or in the days before computers, use sign language to try and communicate with children.

★

The following morning when Shazia had gone to school, I got a phone call from my supervising social worker Becky at the agency.

'How are you doing?' she asked. 'I hear that the teenager you had over the weekend is staying a bit longer now.'

'Yes, that's right,' I said.

'Has her social worker put a time frame on it?' she replied. 'Do you know how long she's going to be with you? I know the social worker mentioned that there were suspicions of a forced marriage, but do you know what's going on?'

'To be honest I have absolutely no idea,' I admitted. 'At the moment it's just a gut feeling from the social worker that something isn't right, as both Shazia and her parents are denying everything now.'

'Well, as you and I know, it's going to take something more than a gut feeling to keep a child in care,' Becky sighed. 'She'll need something more concrete if Shazia is going to stay with you.'

'I know,' I told her. 'Rachel's going to take a view after the next contact session tomorrow.'

'Well keep me posted,' Becky replied before saying goodbye.

Talking of Rachel, half an hour later she was on my doorstep clutching a large brown holdall.

'I've brought round some clothes for Shazia from her parents,' she said when I answered the door to let her in. 'I'm happy for you to have a quick rummage through it to check there's nothing of concern in there.'

It was something I always liked to do before passing on a bag to a child, as in the past I'd found everything from notes and money to razorblades and drugs in the stuff that parents had sent for their children.

The bag from Shazia's parents contained nothing but clothes. There was some plain underwear, a couple of long-sleeved nightdresses and five or six shalwar kameez and some long scarves. For some reason, I'd expected brightly coloured, embroidered clothes but these were all drab brown, grey or black. There were no personal items or toiletries, make-up or jewellery that you might expect a fourteen-year-old girl to have.

'I spoke to Shazia's parents about the things that you raised with me the other day,' said Rachel. 'They don't want her to go out and meet friends or go out on her own unsupervised. I've agreed that an adult always has to be with her.'

'OK,' I said. 'That's fine by me.'

To be honest, after what had happened at the weekend with Shazia missing her curfew, I would have felt anxious at letting her out on her own again.

'If she does want to see Zeena or another friend after school, then there's no reason why they can't come round here,' Rachel suggested.

'The other thing is that they don't want her to watch any television,' she added, raising her eyebrows.

'That's a difficult one as there are two other people in this house who watch TV,' I told her, exasperated. 'If Louisa's watching something in the evening, it seems unfair to have to ask her to turn it off or make Shazia leave the room.

'I'll always make sure that she's watching something age-appropriate,' I decided. 'But banning TV completely is going to be rather tricky.'

'Just do the best you can, Maggie,' Rachel said patiently. 'I know it will help reassure her parents and put their minds at rest.

'Oh, I also mentioned the toilet thing,' she added. 'Mum said Shazia has no medical conditions and that she likes to be clean so she's probably just washing her hands.'

'Oh, OK,' I said, doubtfully, although I wasn't convinced that anyone would spend twenty minutes washing their hands.

That afternoon when Shazia came home from school I showed her the bag that her parents had sent. She didn't seem that pleased to have her own things, however.

'Does that mean I can't wear the clothes you bought me any more?' she asked, looking crestfallen. 'Because I really like them.'

'I don't see why not,' I told her. 'As long as it's alongside your usual clothes. It's probably not a good idea to wear the clothes we bought to the contact session tomorrow. In fact, if you want to get changed at school again, why don't you take one of the shalwar kameez and wear that?' I suggested.

I was keen for things to go smoothly and I knew her parents would appreciate seeing her in her own clothes.

'OK,' she sighed reluctantly.

The following day I picked Shazia up after school after dropping Michael off with my friend Vicky, who was a fellow foster carer.

Thankfully, when we pulled up to the contact centre there was no sign of Shazia's brother Adil, and Shazia seemed a lot less apprehensive as we entered the building.

Rachel was there to meet us when we walked in.

'This is Foz, who's going to interpret things for us,' she said, introducing us to a kind-looking woman in her fifties.

'Foz works for Social Services and she speaks fluent Punjabi so she's offered to help out today.'

As soon as we walked into the contact room, Mr Bains jumped up and held his arms out to Shazia. She hesitated at first, unsure, and then went towards him.

As he hugged her, he spoke to her in Punjabi.

Rachel looked across at Foz.

'He's saying how much he's missed his beautiful daughter and how he forgives her for telling lies. He's telling her how all he wants is for her to come back home to her loving family where she belongs.'

Rachel and I looked at each other, surprised. This was totally different from the raised voices and angry conversations I'd seen at the last contact.

When Shazia's father had released her from her hug, she went straight over to her mother, who reached out and put her hands on Shazia's cheeks, smiling at her as she spoke to her in Punjabi.

'She's saying that they have all missed their beautiful daughter so much,' said Foz, translating for us. 'She's saying that everything will be OK and they want Shazia to come home.'

'I love you, Mamma,' said Shazia, with tears in her eyes, cuddling close to her mother.

The rest of the session passed calmly. This time, it was a picture of family unity and devotion with both of Shazia's parents telling her how much they loved her and begging her to come home. They were both a lot friendlier to me too.

'Maggie, thank you so much for looking after our daughter,' Mr Bains told me, smiling broadly as we got up to leave.

I was taken aback by the sudden change that seemed to have taken place.

On the way home Shazia seemed delighted.

'They're not cross with me any more and they really want me back,' she smiled happily. 'When can I go home, Maggie? I just want to go home now.'

'I'll talk to Rachel this evening,' I promised, although I couldn't help but feel a little suspicious at the sudden change in her parents' behaviour.

Later on, when Shazia was in bed, Rachel rang me.

'Well that was very different to the last contact session,' I told her. 'Shazia was very happy when she left.'

'It was like being with a different family,' agreed Rachel. 'But Maggie, did it feel genuine to you?'

Contact is usually held in an unfamiliar place with strangers observing parents' behaviour and the way that they interact with their children. Parents are conscious that every single move they make and every word they say is going to watched and scrutinised. How could it ever feel natural?

'It's always going to be a bit forced,' I said. 'That's the whole nature of contact.'

'I know what you mean, but I still have that niggling feeling,' Rachel replied. 'It all felt a bit staged to me.'

'A niggling feeling isn't enough to keep a child in care, Rachel,' I told her sadly.

'You're right,' she sighed. 'I don't know who or what to believe any more.'

Rachel had organised a meeting at Social Services on Friday to assess where we were with the case.

'Also, just to let you know Shazia has invited her friend Zeena round for tea after school tomorrow,' I told her. 'She asked if they could go out somewhere so I explained it would have to be here. I thought it might cheer her up.'

'That's fine,' said Rachel. 'Thanks for letting me know and I'll see you on Friday.'

The following day I picked up Shazia and Zeena after school.

'I've never come back with Shaz after school before,' said Zeena excitedly, as the girls climbed into the car.

'Why's that?' I asked, surprised.

'Oh, my mum and dad don't like me having anyone round to the house,' Shazia replied matter-of-factly.

It was sweet to see how excited these two teenagers were about spending a couple of hours together after school. They played with Michael and when Louisa got in from work she braided their hair.

Zeena's mum Naz came to pick her up later that evening. She was in her forties and was wearing jeans and a blouse with a scarf around her neck and shoulders.

'Thank you for letting Zeena come round,' she said when I answered the door. 'She was so excited. The girls have never been allowed to spend any time together after school and they've been friends for years. I've phoned Mr and Mrs Bains countless times to ask if they would allow Shazia to come to our house, but they never have. I think perhaps they think we're too Western for their liking,' she added, raising her eyebrows at me.

'It's a pleasure,' I smiled, meaning it. 'The girls have had a great time.'

The more I heard about Shazia's home life, the more surprised I was about how little freedom she had. Her parents were obviously very strict about what they allowed her to do and it was totally different to most teenagers that I had come across.

The following day, I headed to Social Services for the meeting about Shazia. Vicky had offered to look after Michael again so I dropped him off after I'd driven Shazia to school.

Becky was coming along as well as myself, Rachel and Rachel's manager Angela.

'Just to have a quick recap. As you all know, Shazia, who is fourteen and comes from a Pakistani Muslim background, has been in care for a week after we brought her in last Friday on an EPO,' said Rachel as we all settled down around the table.

'She had allegedly told a friend at school that her parents were taking her to Pakistan against her will and forcing her into an arranged marriage.

'Subsequently the police confirmed that three plane tickets had been booked. However, the family denied the accusation of a forced marriage, claiming that the flights were for a relative's wedding that they were attending, coming back here three or four days later.'

'So where are we at with everything now?' asked Angela.

'I've spoken to both Shazia and her parents several times since then and no new information has come to light,' said Rachel. 'Shazia claims she made it all up to get back at her parents for being strict and her parents are saying the same thing.'

'How did the second contact session go?' said Angela.

'The contact session yesterday couldn't have been more different to the first one,' Rachel told her. 'Dad and Mum were saying how much they miss Shazia, how they've forgiven her and they want her home.

'Everyone was saying the right things,' continued Rachel. 'But personally I've still got a gut feeling that everything's not as it should be.'

'While you might have a gut feeling, Rachel, we don't actually have anything to go on here,' said Angela firmly. 'There's no concrete evidence to suggest the forced marriage allegations were true or that Shazia is in any immediate danger. If we don't actually have anything more substantial to go on and if both sides are saying they want her to go home, we don't really have much choice.'

'Maggie, is this what Shazia really wants?' Becky asked, turning to me.

'That's what she's telling me,' I replied. 'She insists that she made up the story about the forced marriage and she keeps asking when she can go home. I know her parents are strict, but she's not mentioned anything that I would class as neglect, violence or cruelty. She did have some bruising to her face and neck when she arrived, but perhaps we have to accept her explanation that she walked into a kitchen cupboard.'

'I don't think we have any other option but to let Shazia go back home, in that case,' said Angela matter-of-factly. 'All we can put this down to is teenage silliness. This young lady was obviously trying to create a bit of drama to impress her friend.'

I could see Rachel wasn't convinced that this was the right decision, but Social Services' hands were tied. Although

Shazia's parents had booked flights to Pakistan, we had to trust that they were telling the truth about going to a family wedding. There was nothing concrete to justify keeping Shazia in the care system at this point. Shazia was saying she wanted to go home, her parents were saying they wanted her home, and nothing had been raised to stop that from happening.

We had to believe Shazia that she had made up the story about being forced into a wedding she didn't want. Whether that was for attention or to get back at her parents, we might never know. Perhaps it was just a clash between traditional parents and a daughter who wanted to embrace the Western world and wasn't allowed to. Whatever it was, we had reached the end of the line. After a week in care, Shazia was finally going home.

FIVE

Homecoming

By the end of the meeting it was decided that Shazia could go home the following day.

'Umm, it's Saturday tomorrow so I won't be working,' said Rachel apologetically.

'I'm sure a duty social worker could take her,' replied Angela brusquely.

'It's OK, I'll do it,' I told them quickly. 'Rachel, when you speak to her parents, why don't you tell them that I'll drop her off with them tomorrow morning.'

'Thank you, Maggie,' said Angela. 'That's much appreciated.'

It didn't seem right having a duty social worker that Shazia had never met taking her home. It had been an unsettling week for her and I thought it was better that it was someone she knew in case there were any last-minute wobbles or concerns.

'What about Michael?' asked Becky.

'I'll check with Louisa, but I'm sure she won't mind looking after him while I take Shazia home.'

The rest of the meeting was spent tying up loose ends.

'We'll keep the case open for the next month or so to see how things go,' said Angela. 'Rachel, perhaps you could make another couple of visits to the family when Shazia's back just to make sure everything seems OK. If all seems fine, then we'll close the case.'

'Yes, of course I'm more than happy to do that,' she nodded.

'When do you want to tell Shazia?' I asked Rachel, once the meeting had ended.

'I can come round when she gets back from school this afternoon,' she replied. 'In the meantime I'm going to go and update her parents.'

'Good luck,' I told her. 'At least you're bringing them good news this time so they might be more friendly.'

On the way home I stopped off at Vicky's to pick up Michael. As soon as she opened the door he toddled towards me, his little fists filled with Play-Doh.

'Someone looks happy,' I laughed, scooping him up and kissing his dark curls.

'Oh, he's had a whale of a time,' smiled Vicky. 'He's been as good as gold. How did your meeting go?' she asked.

'OK,' I said. 'They've decided that Shazia can go home tomorrow.'

'Blimey, that was quick,' she gasped. 'She hasn't been with you long at all.'

'Just a week,' I shrugged.

I couldn't help but think about what a strange seven days it had been.

'So did they get to the bottom of the forced marriage allegations in the end?' she asked.

'Not really,' I sighed. 'No one's sure about who or what to believe. Social Services have got nothing concrete to go on, so we have to believe that Shazia made the whole thing up.'

'Well, there's nothing teenagers like more than a bit of drama and to get at their parents,' Vicky said thoughtfully. 'But it's a strange thing to make up.'

I completely agreed with her. All I could hope was that we were doing the right thing by sending Shazia back home.

The afternoon flew by and it wasn't long before it was time to collect Shazia from school. As I pulled up outside my house, Rachel was already waiting on the doorstep.

'What does she want now?' sighed Shazia. 'I only saw her yesterday.'

'Give her a chance,' I told her as I unbuckled Michael from his car seat. 'She obviously wants to talk to you about something important.'

We all went through to the kitchen and I settled Michael in his playpen and flicked the kettle on while a reluctant-looking Shazia sat at the table with Rachel.

'I've got some news for you,' Rachel told her, smiling. 'I had a meeting with my manager today and we had a chat about you and your parents and what's been happening this week.'

She paused and Shazia looked at her expectantly, her brow furrowed.

'We've decided that if you feel OK about it, then we're happy for you to go home tomorrow.'

Shazia looked confused.

'Are you messing with me?' she asked, frowning at Rachel. 'I can go home? Tomorrow?'

'Yes, you can go back to live with your parents,' smiled Rachel. 'I've told them that Maggie is going to drop you home in the morning. Is that what you want?'

'Yes,' grinned Shazia, barely able to believe it. 'Yes. That's brilliant. I'm going to go upstairs now and start packing my stuff.'

Before she could say another word, Shazia had rushed out of the kitchen and upstairs.

'Well, she seemed delighted,' I said, once Shazia had left the room. 'What did her parents say when you told them?'

'They were pleased, of course,' Rachel nodded. 'But Mr Bains was ranting about how we'd wasted their time and taken Shazia into care for no reason.'

Part of me could understand their anger. Having Social Services becoming involved with your family is very intrusive and parents inevitably feel like it's a criticism of them and their parenting, which a lot of the time, it is. There's also a real stigma attached to it and parents feel very ashamed at the thought of other people finding out.

'At least Shazia is happy,' I replied. 'What do you think about her going home?'

'You know what I think, Maggie,' sighed Rachel. 'My instincts are telling me this isn't the last we've seen of this girl.'

For Shazia's sake I hoped that Rachel was wrong. I still didn't know what to make of it. All I could hope was that if her parents really had been planning to take her to Pakistan and force her into an arranged marriage, then this had scared them enough that they'd think twice about trying to do the same thing again.

Before Rachel left, she called Shazia down to see her.

'I'm not going to be around tomorrow, so Maggie's going to take you home in the morning,' she told her. 'You know you can get hold of me via your school if there's a problem and I'll still be popping in to see you over the next few weeks at your parents' to check everything's going OK.'

'Alright,' Shazia smiled distractedly before heading back upstairs. She was clearly more interested in getting on with her packing than any lingering goodbye with Rachel.

'I hope it goes OK tomorrow, Maggie, and I'll be in touch,' Rachel said, turning to leave. 'It's been nice working with you.'

'Likewise,' I replied.

When Rachel had left, I picked up Michael and carried him upstairs to see how Shazia was getting on. I noticed that she'd packed all the clothes that her parents had sent, but she'd left the pyjamas, tops and leggings that I'd bought.

'You're welcome to take those with you,' I told her, indicating the neat pile still folded up in the drawer. 'I bought them for you to keep, you know.'

'There isn't any point,' she sighed. 'My parents won't let me wear them and they'll just make me throw them away.'

'No problem,' I nodded, keen to avoid saying anything critical about her parents. 'I'll keep them here. You never know, I might have another teenage girl arrive on my doorstep who needs them.'

She gave me a weak smile. I put Michael down on the floor and sat on the bed next to her.

'I know it's been a hard week for you, but it's over now,' I told her. 'You must be so pleased to be going home.'

'It's been weird, but it's been OK,' she smiled. 'I've liked being at your house. I like the clothes you got me and having Zee over and meeting Louisa and Michael, but I missed my mum.'

'And I'm sure she's missed you too,' I soothed.

That night when Louisa got home from work, we all sat down to pizza and chips.

'Louisa, guess what happened today?' Shazia told her excitedly. 'I found out that I'm going home tomorrow.'

'Are you?' Louisa replied, surprised, glancing over at me to check that Shazia had got her facts right.

'Yes, I'm going to drop her back in the morning,' I nodded.

'Ooh, how does that feel?' asked Louisa. 'Are you looking forward to it or will it feel a bit strange?'

'Nah, I'm pleased,' Shazia grinned.

'I will miss you all though,' she added, shyly.

As if he was giving us his thoughts on the matter, Michel started babbling and threw his pizza and beaker of water on the floor.

'Don't tell me you're going to miss this?' laughed Louisa.

'I am a bit,' she smiled.

'I don't believe it,' I teased. 'I'll bet she'll have forgotten us by this time next week, Louisa.'

I wanted to keep things light-hearted and at least it made Shazia smile.

In the morning, as soon as we'd finished breakfast, Shazia was ready to go, the brown bag from her parents slung over her shoulder.

'All set?' I asked her.

'Yep, I think so,' she nodded.

'Bye Michael,' she smiled, dropping down to the floor and holding his little hands.

He gave her a cheeky grin and then ran off to play with his train set.

'See you, Shazia,' said Louisa, giving her a hug.

'Thanks for showing me how to braid my hair and for being nice to me,' Shazia mumbled, her cheeks a little pink.

'That's OK,' Louisa grinned.

'Thank you for watching Michael, lovey,' I told her. 'I'll be as quick as I can.'

'There's no rush,' she said. 'I'm not going to Charlie's until this afternoon so take as long as you need to.'

It was at times like this that I really appreciated having Louisa around. It would be much easier dropping Shazia home without a bored and restless toddler fussing in the car.

Even though I knew she was pleased to be going home, Shazia was very quiet during the 40-minute drive back to her parents' house and I could tell she was nervous. The suburb where the Bains lived was a predominantly Asian community and I'd never been there before. As I drove down the main high street, there were butchers selling halal meat and clothes shops selling saris in every colour of the rainbow along with rolls of beautifully embroidered fabric. It was only the other side of town from me but it felt like a different world.

'This is it,' said Shazia as we pulled up outside a red-brick back-to-back terrace. The front steps led up to a door on the first floor and I could see that it had a basement and a loft.

'It's a big house,' I said.

'It needs to be,' she replied. 'My two brothers still live at home and my aunt and uncle live with us.'

I suspected that Shazia's parents wouldn't want me to go into the house so I said my goodbyes in the car.

'I won't have time to come in, lovey, as I've got to get back so Louisa can go to Charlie's.

'But you've got my number, so if there are any problems or you need me, just give me a ring.'

'OK,' she said, giving me a weak smile. 'I'm sure I'll be fine.'

'It was lovely having you with us and getting to know you a little bit,' I told her, giving her a hug.

'Thank you, Maggie,' she said. 'Thanks for everything.'

I got her bag out of the boot and walked up the front steps with her. Shazia knocked hesitantly on the door.

Her dad promptly answered the door with her mum standing close behind him.

'Shazia!' she beamed, and Shazia rushed to her and fell into her arms.

'Thank you for bringing her back,' said Mr Bains abruptly. 'She's home now.'

I didn't even have time to reply before he closed the door in my face. It was a shock, but in a way I didn't blame him. He was desperate to get me out of there as quickly as possible. He saw me as part of Social Services – the people who had taken their daughter away from them. It's something you learn to get used to over the years. They'd got their daughter back and now they wanted to move forward. Why would they want to welcome me into their home?

When I got back, Louisa was playing with Michael in the kitchen.

'That was quick,' she said, surprised. 'How did it go?'

'Oh, it was fine,' I told her. 'You know I like quick good-byes. I didn't hang around.'

The rest of the weekend passed very quietly. Louisa was at Charlie's so it was just Michael and I. On Sunday afternoon, while Michael was having a nap, I went into the spare room to strip the bed Shazia had slept in. As I put the pile of clothes she'd left into a cupboard on the landing, I couldn't help but wonder how she was getting on.

I hoped she had settled back in at home OK. Above all, I hoped that she was safe. There was nothing to suggest other-wise and I had seen with my own eyes how happy she was to be reunited with her mother so I had to believe it.

On Monday morning Becky called me.

'Did Shazia get off OK?' she asked.

'Yep, I took her back on Saturday morning,' I replied. 'Rachel's going to keep in touch and let me know how she is.'

'Good,' she said.

'Well, there's no rest for the wicked I'm afraid,' she joked. 'I'll put you back on the available list so I'm sure it won't be long until another placement comes up. I'm also ringing to tell you that Michael's social worker Helen is going to get in touch with you today.'

'How come?' I asked, hoping nothing had happened to Kerry.

'She wants to arrange a planning meeting to talk about Michael going back to live with Kerry full time and how we're going to do that.'

'Oh, I didn't expect that to happen so soon,' I said, surprised.

I knew Kerry was feeling a lot stronger but I thought it would be another few months at least before we started to talk about Michael returning to her care full time.

'Helen said she's making good progress, the solo contact has been going really well and the community mental health team are pleased with her,' Becky replied.

I was really happy for Kerry. I just had to get my head around the fact that, after almost a year at my house, Michael would be leaving for good.

I knew Louisa would be upset to see him go, but I decided not to mention it until we'd finalised a definite timescale.

A couple of days later we held the planning meeting about Michael at Social Services. Becky was there as well as Kerry and Helen and a community mental health worker called Nina.

Kerry looked so happy.

'I can't believe this is finally happening, Maggie,' she grinned.

'We're going to take things very slowly and make sure you and Michael are both happy and settled,' said Helen. 'But everyone is really pleased with how things are going and the amazing progress that you've made.

'Your contact worker says you're doing brilliantly,' she added, looking through the notes. 'What's it been like having Michael on your own for a few hours?'

'I've really loved it,' Kerry nodded. 'I've been knackered afterwards but it's been nice to feel like a proper mum again.'

Helen suggested upping the level of contact to three days and letting Michael stay overnight with Kerry once a week.

'We'll look at things in another month and if it's all going well, we can look at Michael coming back to live with you full time.'

Kerry burst into tears.

I put my arm around her and I could feel her bony shoulders shaking with sobs.

'Is that OK, Kerry?' I asked. 'Is that too much, do you think?'

'If an overnight visit every week is too much for you to cope with, we don't have to do that straight away,' Helen reassured her.

'No, no, I want to,' she insisted, smiling through her tears. 'I'm crying because I'm so happy. All I've ever wanted is to get Michael back to live with me. That's the only thing that's kept me going while I've been ill. I honestly do feel ready to have him back. He's been without his mummy for too long.'

'I'm sorry, Maggie,' she sniffed. 'I know you're going to miss him.'

'Of course I am,' I smiled. 'He's a gorgeous boy but he's *your* gorgeous boy and he's going back where he belongs.'

Kerry had been through a lot, but she had fought so hard to get well again and I knew she desperately wanted her son back. I was willing to support her in any way I could.

'Shall we start the overnight visit this week then?' suggested Helen.

'Yes, that would be great,' said Kerry, drying her eyes.

'That's fine by me,' I agreed.

We arranged that Michael would stay over on Friday night with Kerry.

That morning, I got a few of his toys and some other bits together so he'd have a few familiar things around him.

Kerry had lost her flat when she'd gone into hospital and the council had recently given her a new place. Michael had been there for contact but he'd never lived there.

'Come in,' she smiled when she saw us at the door. The flat was small but Kerry kept it immaculately clean.

'Since the meeting I've spent every waking moment trying to sort out his bedroom,' she said. 'I wanted to make it nice for him.'

She took me in to have a look.

'Oh Kerry, it's absolutely beautiful,' I gasped.

It was all pale blue and mustard yellow and there was a mural of a tree on the wall, woodland-themed bedding and a wardrobe and chest of drawers stenciled with leaves and flowers.

'You must have worked so hard doing all this.'

'I wanted it to be nice for him,' she said proudly, blushing a little. 'I gave it a lick of paint and bought a stencilling kit.'

I stayed for a quick cup of tea but I was keen to leave and let Kerry give Michael his tea and get him settled before it was bedtime.

As soon as I put my coat on to leave, Michael came toddling over and held his arms out to me.

'Up, up,' he babbled, his eyes wide.

He obviously thought he was coming back with me.

'You're staying with Mummy tonight, sweetie,' I told him gently.

I picked him up and gave him a kiss and a cuddle and then I handed him back to Kerry. But as soon as he was in her arms he started struggling and wriggling, his little arms outstretched as he tried desperately to come back to me.

'He wants to leave with you,' sighed Kerry, her eyes full of hurt. 'He doesn't want to stay with me. He's more attached to you than me.'

'It's more about the fact that he spends the majority of his time with me,' I soothed. 'He knows that you're his mummy and he's going to be absolutely fine with you.'

I knew it was hard for Kerry to see her son wanting to go with me, but it was about ages and stages. Babies tended to get very clingy from around their first birthdays.

'Remember it's a big period of change for Michael as well as you,' I reassured her. 'It will take a little bit of time for you to both get used to the new routine.'

'I know,' nodded Kerry, looking uncertain.

'Now I'm going to go so you can enjoy your night with your son,' I smiled. 'Don't worry, he'll be fine.'

As I drove home, I remembered Louisa was at Charlie's. So for the first time in what was possibly years, I was at home alone without any children. The house felt eerily quiet as I walked in, but I was determined to enjoy the peace and quiet as I knew it wasn't going to last for long.

SIX

Party Then Panic

All the developments with Michael had taken my mind off of Shazia, which was probably a good thing. It had distracted me from worrying about her and wondering how her first few days back at home were going.

Thankfully, Michael's first overnight stay with Kerry was a success. He was pleased to see me the next day, but she said he'd been settled and had slept well and everyone seemed happy for the same thing to happen again the following week.

The next few days were strange for me, as for once in my fostering career, I'd hit a quiet patch. It was unusual because there were no new placements on the horizon, not even any respite care, and with Michael spending more and more time having contact with Kerry, I had a fair bit of time to myself.

'It feels weird,' I told Becky when I spoke to her.

'Just enjoy the break, Maggie,' she laughed. 'You know it's not going to last long. Spend some time with Graham, go and watch a film or read a book.'

Graham was the man I'd been dating for the past eighteen months or so. He was a physiotherapist in his early forties. He was everything that I looked for in a man – tall, salt and pepper hair, and he was a kind and gentle person. He understood that my fostering meant I didn't have much time for a social life and he never put any pressure on me to see him.

It would be nice to have some time with him and I couldn't remember the last time I'd been to the cinema without a child in tow. As for a book, I'd started one about a year ago and I still hadn't got any further than the first chapter.

It was lovely to be able to enjoy a coffee in the daytime with Graham and one evening when Michael was on his overnight stay with Kerry, we went out for a meal.

'This is a novelty,' he smiled. 'In the entire time I've known you I don't think I've ever seen you so much.'

'I know,' I sighed. 'I'm sorry I'm so unavailable most of the time.'

'I understand,' he smiled. 'I'm only teasing. When we first started seeing each other, you were very upfront about your fostering. I understand that it's a 24/7 commitment and I know you wouldn't want it any other way.

'That's what I love about you, Maggie,' he added. 'Your devotion to every single child that comes through your door. I know you want to do the best for each and every one of them and I completely admire that.'

I reached across the table and grabbed his hand.

'Thank you,' I blushed. 'That's a lovely thing to say. You're right, fostering isn't one of those 9–5 jobs. It is my entire life and it's exhausting and frustrating and upsetting at times, but

I wouldn't want to do anything else. But I really do wish I could spend some more time with you.'

'Me too,' replied Graham, having a sip of his beer. 'It's nice to be able to make plans and go out like a normal couple.'

'Don't get used to it,' I teased. 'It could all change tomorrow with one phone call.'

I did get a call the following day, but it wasn't what I was expecting. A number flashed up on my mobile that I recognised as Social Services'. I assumed it was about a new placement so I was confused when I heard Rachel's voice.

'Hi Maggie,' she said. 'I thought I'd give you a quick ring about Shazia.'

'Why?' I asked nervously. 'What's happened?'

'Nothing to worry about at all,' she reassured me. 'The opposite in fact.'

It had been ten days since Shazia had left and Rachel explained that she'd called round to her parent's house to check how they were doing.

'Everything seemed absolutely fine,' Rachel told me. 'Dad was chatty, quite pleasant even. I saw Shazia when she got back from school.'

'How was she?' I asked.

'A bit quiet,' she said. 'She didn't say much, but her parents let me have a word with her on her own and she said she was OK.'

'That's great,' I said, relieved. 'So nothing raised any concerns?'

'Nothing at all,' Rachel replied. 'Shazia seemed happy enough. I honestly think I got it wrong, Maggie. They seemed fine. Anyway, I said I'd pop in again in a couple of weeks and then we'd look at closing the case.'

'That's great,' I said. 'Let me know when you do, just to put my mind at rest once and for all. I've been thinking about her, wondering how she was getting on.'

'I will, Maggie,' she assured me. 'I'll be in touch.'

It was a relief to hear that everything had settled down for Shazia. I made a mental note to tell Louisa when she got home that night as she had been asking about how Shazia was doing.

Later that afternoon I got a text from Louisa.

Hi, Can I bring Charlie round 4 tea 2nite?

Charlie often came round for dinner, but it was normally at the weekend when he and Louisa weren't at work. It was an ordinary Tuesday night so I wasn't doing anything particularly fancy.

I tapped out a reply.

Course you can. Hope he's OK with chicken kiev. See you later xx

When Louisa got home from work that night I was in the kitchen setting the table and Michael was playing with his toys on the floor.

'Maggie?' she called from the hallway. 'We're back.'

'I'm in the kitchen,' I yelled.

When she walked in with Charlie I was surprised to see her clutching a bottle of Prosecco.

'Bubbles on a Tuesday?' I laughed. 'What's the special occasion? It can't be my chicken kiev.'

Louisa glanced at Charlie. They gave each other a knowing look and her cheeks flushed red.

'We've got something to tell you, Maggie,' she said, breathlessly.

She paused then she grabbed Charlie's hand.

'Me and Charlie got engaged. It happened at the weekend, but I didn't want to tell you until we'd got the ring. He picked it up from the jeweller's today. Look. . .'

She held out her left hand and showed me the gold band studded with three little diamonds.

'It's nothing fancy but I love it,' she beamed.

I was so stunned, I couldn't speak at first. They'd taken me completely by surprise.

'Oh my goodness,' I gasped, staring at her ring. 'That's lovely news. I'm so, so happy for you, flower.'

I gave Louisa a big hug and much to his embarrassment, Charlie too.

'That's wonderful,' I grinned, my eyes filling with tears. 'Come on then, let's crack open that bottle.'

The news had been a shock, but I was genuinely pleased for them. Louisa was almost twenty-one, but she had a wise head on her young shoulders. Charlie, with his boy-band hairstyle and his designer trainers, was a couple of years older and he was a lovely lad. He had a stable job as a mechanic and I could tell by the adoring way he looked at her that he would do absolutely anything for Louisa.

Before we tucked into our meal, we had a toast.

'Congratulations,' I said, clinking glasses. 'I'm so happy for you both.'

As we ate dinner, we chit-chatted about their plans.

'Don't most youngsters live together first before they decide to tie the knot?' I asked them.

'Charlie wanted to do things properly,' said Louisa. 'But now we're engaged, I think we might start looking for some-where and move in together in a couple of months.'

Charlie still lived at home with his parents.

As I sat and listened to them talking excitedly about the kind of flat that they'd like, a sudden realisation hit me.

Louisa would be moving out.

It was a bittersweet moment for me. I was so, so happy for Louisa. After the trauma of losing her parents as a teenager, she'd been so strong and brave. She was living her life and doing everything she wanted to do. She had a job and a boyfriend whom she loved and she was growing up and spreading her wings. She was brilliant with children and I knew she was going to make a fantastic mum one day. However, another part of me, the selfish part, couldn't help but think that she was my little girl and that I didn't want her to leave. I couldn't love Louisa any more than if I had given birth to her myself and in my eyes, she *was* my daughter. It was going to feel really strange not having her around.

That night when Charlie had gone, Louisa helped me clear up the dishes.

'You are pleased for me aren't you, Maggie?' she asked nervously.

'Of course I am, lovey,' I reassured her. 'You took me by surprise that's all, but I'm delighted. I like Charlie, you know I do, and I can see how happy he makes you. I'm just going to miss you when you go.'

'Don't worry,' she grinned. 'It'll probably take us ages to find a flat we both like and that we can afford and even when we get one, I bet I'll be back here all the time.'

'I'll hold you to that,' I smiled.

'Plus you've got little Michael to keep you company,' she added, watching him toddle around the kitchen.

'Hopefully he'll be back living with his mother soon,' I said. 'I don't think it's going to be long before he goes home.'

A flash of an idea suddenly came to me.

'How about I organise a little engagement party for you?' I suggested. 'I've got a bit of time on my hands at the moment. We could have a few friends and Charlie's parents round to celebrate?'

'Yes, that would be great,' she smiled.

'How about a week on Friday? I'll do a bit of a buffet.'

'As long as you're sure, that would be brilliant,' she told me, giving me a hug. 'Thank you, Maggie.'

That night I went to bed with a happy but slightly heavy heart. Change was always hard but I knew in the long run it was good. Louisa had to make her own life and her own family and hopefully she knew that she would always be part of mine.

On the days Michael was with Kerry, and with no new placements arriving, I threw myself into sorting out the engagement party. I did a big supermarket shop for the drinks and food and I got some decorations and a cake. My friend Vicky was coming along as well as our other family friends, Anne and Bob, and Wendy, whom Louisa had known for as long as she had known me. Becky had also said she'd pop in, as over the years she'd got to know Louisa too and she was an important part of my fostering. Even Graham, who was normally so shy about meeting any of my friends, agreed to pop in. I didn't know Charlie's parents, Jan and Adam, very well, but I'd met them a couple of times and they'd agreed to come along.

Kerry had Michael staying with her overnight on the day of the party, so I could focus on getting everything ready. I was a nervous wreck. I'd been running around all day and I didn't have anything to wear, but thankfully it went well and everyone had fun celebrating the good news. Louisa had a great time and although Charlie looked a bit embarrassed by all the attention, he went along with it.

'It's going to be a bit of a change for you,' said Becky as we sat down together and tucked into a piece of engagement cake.

'I know,' I sighed. 'It's going to take a bit of getting used to, but it's worth it to see Louisa so happy.'

By eleven all the guests had finally gone. I said a quick goodbye to Graham and when I came back in, Louisa and Charlie had started clearing up.

'I'll sort this out,' I told them, shooing them away. 'It's your party, you shouldn't be clearing up. Why don't you get yourselves back to Charlie's?'

'Are you sure?' asked Louisa.

'Positive,' I smiled. 'I hope you've had a good night.'

'It's been brilliant, Maggie,' she beamed. 'Thank you so much for doing this for us.'

'See you tomorrow,' I told her, giving her a hug.

After they'd gone I stared at the dining table full of empty glasses and dirty plates and sighed. I was shattered, but I couldn't bear going to bed until I'd tidied it all away. I knew it would be much worse if I left it until the morning and besides, I could have a rare lie-in if I wanted to as Kerry wasn't dropping Michael back until the afternoon.

I was just rinsing some plates before I put them in the dishwasher when I heard my mobile ringing from the other side of the kitchen.

Who on earth was calling this late on a Friday night?

I didn't make it over to answer it in time and it had clicked onto voicemail by the time I'd picked it up.

I didn't recognise the number on the screen. Before I could listen to the voicemail, it rang again. Whoever it was was obviously eager to get hold of me.

'Hello?' I answered.

'Maggie?' said a woman's voice. 'Is that Maggie?'

'Yes,' I replied hesitantly. 'Who's this?'

'It's Naz,' she said. 'You know, Zeena's mum, Shazia's best friend?'

I could tell something wasn't right by the panicked tone of her voice.

'Hi Naz, how can I help? Is everything OK?'

'No,' she sighed. 'I'm afraid it's not. I've got Shazia here,' she continued. 'She wanted me to call you. She's in a terrible state and she desperately needs your help. She's in danger and I need to get her away from here. My house is the first place her family will come looking for her and I can't risk her being here. I need to get her out of here as quickly as possible. Can I please bring her to yours?'

I couldn't believe what I was hearing.

'Now?' I gasped. 'But what on earth has happened to her?'

'There isn't time to explain,' Naz insisted. 'I need to get her to your house as quickly as I can. We can talk then. We're coming now. I remember where you live from when I picked up Zeena.'

Before I could say another word, she'd hung up.

My heart was hammering in my chest as a million questions ran through my mind. Why was Shazia in danger? What on earth had gone on? The last I'd heard from Rachel everything at home was fine. What had changed? Or was this another case of Shazia making things up to create a bit of drama?

I'd heard the tone of Naz's voice on the phone, though. The desperation and the fear sounded genuine to me.

As quickly as I could, I tidied up the last of the debris from the party and then I paced up and down the kitchen waiting for them to arrive. I was anxious to find out what sort of a state Shazia was in.

It was gone midnight before I heard a gentle knock on the front door. I ran to the hallway and opened it with my heart in my mouth.

A bare-faced Naz was standing on the doorstep in tracksuit bottoms and a baggy jumper. She looked around nervously as if to check that no one was following her.

'Has anyone been here asking for Shazia?' she asked immediately.

'No,' I frowned. 'No one knows this address.'

'Come on girls,' she hissed and behind her in the darkness I saw two figures emerge from behind a bush. I could just make out Shazia clinging onto Zeena.

'Come in,' I told them, ushering them into the hallway.

As they stepped into the light, I saw Shazia properly for the first time.

'Oh lovey, what on earth has happened to you?' I gasped.

She looked up at me, her big dark eyes filled with fear, and started sobbing.

'They lied to me, Maggie,' she whimpered. 'It was all a lie.'

She was in a terrible state. Despite it being a mild summer's night, she was shivering and shaking. She was wearing a dirty nightdress with a hoodie over the top and a pair of trainers that were too big for her. Her legs were covered in cuts and were bleeding. She looked thinner than ever and her face was all bruised.

'I had to get out of there,' she babbled. 'If they find me they're really going to kill me this time.'

She was trembling and gasping for breath.

'Shazia, I need you to take big deep breaths and try and stay calm,' I soothed.

I led her into the living room and I noticed Naz behind me checking the front door was locked before turning the hall light off. She seemed genuinely terrified.

Zeena and I helped Shazia over to the sofa and sat her down. Her body was shaking with big gulping sobs.

'It's OK, Shaz, you're safe now,' sighed Zeena, doing her best to try and comfort her friend. 'You're with Maggie now. Everything's going to be alright.'

'Shazia, I'm going to go into the kitchen and get you a drink,' I told her gently. 'I'll be back in a minute, OK?'

She nodded shakily.

'And when I get back and you've calmed down, then I need you to talk to me. I need you to tell me what's happened.'

Shazia nodded again, her head against Zeena's shoulder.

As I walked to the kitchen, my head was spinning. I didn't know what had happened tonight, but it was clear something had gone dreadfully wrong and Shazia was scared. Scared for her life, in fact.

SEVEN

A Safe Haven

When I returned with a glass of water, Shazia was sitting on the sofa still shaking like a leaf. Her breathing was laboured and I suspected that she was having a panic attack.

'Here, have a drink, lovey,' I said, passing her the cup. 'That might help.'

I noticed her lips were all cracked and dry and she gulped down the water in record speed.

I sat down next to her on the sofa and rubbed her back gently.

'Take some big deep breaths,' I soothed. 'There's no need to worry, you're safe now. Nothing's going to happen to you.'

Gradually her breathing became less shallow and slowly she started to calm down.

'That's better,' I sighed. 'You had me worried there.'

Meanwhile, Naz was pacing up and down the living room, looking anxious.

'Maggie, do you mind if we go?' she said quietly. 'If Shazia's family does turn up at our house looking for her and we're

not there, they're going to put two and two together and
assume we're involved. Plus it's late and I want to get Zeena
home to bed.'

'Of course,' I told her. 'I can take things from here.'

'But Mum, I don't wanna go,' Zeena complained. 'Shaz is
in a bad way. I can't leave her.'

'I'll take good care of her,' I reassured her. 'You go home
with your mum and try and get some sleep.'

Reluctantly Zeena got up.

'Shaz, I hope you're OK,' she said, giving her a hug. 'Ring me?'

'OK,' Shazia nodded wearily.

Before she left, Naz gave me her phone number. 'Keep in
touch and let me know how she is.'

'I will do,' I said. 'Once I've talked to Shazia and got to
the bottom of what's happened, I'll phone Social Services.'

I went back into the living room and sat down next to
Shazia.

'So then, sweetie,' I said gently. 'I need you to be very
brave and tell me exactly what has happened.'

Shazia looked up at me, her dark eyes filling with tears
again.

'Please don't be cross, Maggie,' she pleaded. 'But when
I came to stay with you the first time, I lied. What I told
Zeena at school was true. My parents *were* going to take me
to Pakistan and make me get married to my cousin.'

'But why did you change your story and say you'd made
it all up?' I asked her gently. 'We could have helped you.'

'As soon as Zee told the teacher, I got scared,' she mumbled.
'I knew my parents and my brothers would be so angry with
me and I just panicked.

'I'm sorry for lying,' she sobbed, the tears falling down her bruised cheeks. 'I really am. I just didn't know what to do, Maggie.'

'It's OK,' I soothed. 'It doesn't matter. You must have been terrified.'

She nodded shakily.

'At that first contact my dad and my brother were ranting at me in Punjabi about how angry they were with me and how I'd brought shame on our family. They told me to keep my mouth shut and come home.'

In my head I cursed the fact we hadn't had an interpreter there.

'My mum promised me things would be different,' added Shazia. 'She told me if I came home everything would be OK. She said I didn't have to go to Pakistan any more and she promised that she would keep me safe. And I believed her, but she lied, Maggie. She's a stupid bloody liar.'

Her frail body shook with sobs and I put my arm around her.

'Oh lovey,' I sighed. 'I'm so sorry. . . So what happened when you went home?' I pushed on gently. 'Rachel said everything seemed fine when she visited.'

'It was at first,' Shazia nodded. 'Everything was normal again. Then they started talking about us all going to a family wedding in Pakistan.'

She described how her mum had told her one of her cousins was getting married and she had to get measured for a new sari.

'When we were in the shop I overheard Mum talking and I realised that *I* was the bride. It was for *my* wedding.

'They were going to do it again, Maggie,' she cried. 'Mum had lied to me. She'd made me come home and it had all been a lie.'

I could see that of all that had happened to her, this had hurt her the most. Her mum was the one she was closest to and she'd betrayed her.

'All that stuff she told me at the contact – that she loved me and she just wanted her little girl to come home. It was all made up to get me to go back.'

I held her tightly and let her cry it out, stroking her hair gently as my mind whirred. When the tears had subsided, Shazia looked exhausted. But I knew I had to keep her talking and tell me exactly what had happened so that I could call Social Services and give them the full picture.

'Are you OK to go on?' I asked her gently. 'I know it's late and you must be so tired, but I need you to tell me what happened next. Do you think you can do that for me, Shazia?'

She nodded and took a deep breath before she continued her story.

'Now I knew that they were going to try and ship me off to Pakistan and force me to get married, I was frightened but I was angry too. By the time we got home from the shop, I was hysterical. I was screaming and crying at Dad and my brothers, telling them that I wasn't going to go. I wasn't going to get on that plane and I wouldn't go through with it.'

'What did they say?' I asked.

Her eyes filled up again.

'They were angry,' she gulped. 'So, so angry.'

'They said I'd already brought enough shame on our family and that I had to go through with it. They were going to make me. Then they battered me.'

'What, they beat you up?' I asked, horrified to hear that her own family had attacked her.

'My brothers kicked me and punched me, said they were trying to knock some sense into me. Adil held my arm over the gas ring on the cooker and burnt me.'

I felt sick listening to her recount what had happened. It was sadistic, cruel.

'And you know what the worst thing was? Mum just stood there and watched. She let them hurt me. Then they locked me in the basement. That's where I've been until now. They said it was the only way to stop me from telling Zeena again or going to Social Services for help.'

I couldn't believe what I was hearing.

'Oh Shazia,' I sighed.

I couldn't even begin to imagine the fear and the pain that she had gone through, locked down there all alone.

'Do you know how long you were in there?' I asked.

She shrugged.

'Four days, I think,' she mumbled. 'I lost track of what day it was and I didn't have a watch. I had to sleep on a mattress on the floor and they gave me a bucket for a toilet. At first I yelled and I screamed, but after a while I was just so tired and hungry. They gave me bottles of water and a few stale chapattis to eat but nothing else and I just felt so weak and dizzy.'

'What about school?' I asked.

'They rang them and said I was poorly and would be off for a few days. By the time school or Social Services got suspicious, we'd already be in Pakistan.'

As I listened to Shazia's horrific story, I felt furious with myself that we had let her go home and allowed this to happen.

'I'm so sorry, lovey,' I told her. 'I feel like we've let you down.'

'What could you do?' she sighed. 'I was telling you all that I'd made it up. My parents were pretending to be all loving and perfect. There's nothing anyone could have done. You had no reason to keep me in care any more.'

I knew what she was saying was true, but I still felt that I'd failed her in some way. It broke my heart to think of her being beaten up and taken prisoner in her own home by the family who had promised to love and protect her.

'Every day I got more and more desperate, not knowing if that would be the day they were going to take me to Pakistan,' continued Shazia.

'I came up with a plan that if they got me to the airport, I was going to try and do the spoon trick when I went through security.'

'What's that?' I asked, puzzled.

Shazia explained how she'd heard stories about other young Muslim girls who were being taken abroad for forced marriages and had hidden a metal spoon in their underwear.

'They knew if they did that, it would set the alarm off when they went through the metal detector at security,' she explained. 'Then when the security guards pulled them aside they could beg them for help. I thought maybe I could do that, but I didn't know where I was going to find a metal spoon because no one had given me any food.'

'So how on earth did you manage to get out tonight?' I wondered.

'It was Friday and I knew Mum would be at her sister's house and my dad and brothers would be at the mosque for Friday prayers,' she explained. 'I knew my cousin Devinder was round making the curry for dinner like she always does and so I shouted for her and told her that I had stomach cramps and that I desperately needed the loo. I cried and said I couldn't do it in the bucket and I managed to persuade her to let me out so I could go to the toilet. I locked myself in the loo and I managed to climb out of the little window. I only had this nightie on and no shoes, but I knew I had to get out of there before anyone saw me or realised I was gone so I legged it. I just ran and ran until I got to Zeena's house. I knew roughly where she lived, but I'd never been there before and I was so scared I wouldn't find it.'

'How far does Zeena live from you?' I asked.

'Ages,' she sighed. 'It felt like forever to me. At least twenty minutes away. My feet were all cut and bleeding, but I didn't dare stop. I knew as soon as they got home and realised I was gone, they'd come out looking for me.

'It was still daylight when I got near Zeena's. I knew which street it was, but I wasn't sure which house was hers. Then I saw her mum's car in the drive and I knew I'd got the right one.

'But I was scared someone might see me so I hid behind a garage and waited till it got dark, then I ran and knocked on Zee's back door.'

She started trembling again.

'Maggie, if my dad or my brothers find me they'll kill me,' she whispered, looking up at me, her eyes wide with fear.

'That's not going to happen,' I reassured her. 'You're safe here.'

'I swear it's true,' she pleaded. 'You've got to believe me. My brothers said if I ever said anything to anyone again and I didn't go to Pakistan, they would find me and kill me. They said I'd brought enough shame on my family. If I didn't go through with the marriage, I'd destroy my family's honour and standing in the community.

'You know what Adil said would happen if I refused to go to Pakistan and get married? He said he'd force me to take an overdose of pills so it would look like I'd killed myself. What kind of brother would do that?'

It was horrific.

Shazia's whole body was still shaking with fear and I could see that she was genuinely terrified. It was a threat I had to take seriously. I'd read about honour killings where young British women had been murdered by their own family members for going against their wishes and bringing shame or dishonour upon them.

I could see that even the thought of her family finding her had made Shazia panic. Suddenly she jumped up, nervously pulling the net curtain to one side and peering out of the front window into the darkness.

'What if they come here?' she exclaimed, turning to me, her face pale at the thought. 'What if they find me?'

'Did you ever give anyone in your family this address?' I asked her.

She shook her head firmly.

'When I went back home they asked me where your house was, but I promise you, I never told them. I said I didn't recognise the area and I didn't know what street it was because you drove me everywhere.'

I breathed a huge sigh of relief. If they had known where I lived, I would have had to have taken Shazia to another foster carer's house immediately as her safety would have been at risk.

Suddenly my heart stopped as I remembered something. Before Shazia had left, I'd written my phone number down on a piece of paper for her in case she needed to get in touch.

'Shazia, can you remember what you did with my phone number that I wrote down for you?' I asked her nervously.

'Oh, it's OK, it's here,' she mumbled.

She put her hand down her top and fished out a tiny folded-up piece of paper.

'It sounds stupid, but I kept it in my bra,' she smiled. 'I knew it would be safe there and no one would find it.'

'Good girl,' I sighed, relieved. 'There's definitely no way your family can contact me or come round here.'

'What if they look the address up online?' Shazia asked, obviously not convinced.

'Because of my fostering, this house is a secure address,' I reassured her. 'That means it's not in the phone book or on any advertising lists or databases. I don't have a Facebook account or any social media in my name.'

'But what if they drive up and down the streets and they recognise your car?' she continued. 'My parents might have seen it when you dropped me home that day.'

I took her hand.

'Shazia, remember how long it took me to drive you back to your parents' house when you went home?' I told her. 'We were in the car for at least forty minutes. Think of all the streets and houses that we passed on that journey. Hundreds of streets and thousands of houses. Your brothers can't drive up and down every single one of them. Besides, there are lots of scruffy black people carriers around, so they'd have their work cut out recognising mine.

'You have to believe me when I tell you that you're safe, Shazia. They won't find you here and they can't hurt you anymore. I promise.'

'I hope you're right,' she said meekly, tears spilling out of her eyes again.

I looked at the clock. It was just after midnight and I knew I needed to ring my fostering agency and let them know what had happened.

'Are you hungry?' I asked her.

If she'd only lived off a handful of stale chapattis for four days, she must have been starving.

She shook her head.

'Zee's mum gave me some pasta, a packet of crisps and a Twix. I wolfed it down and now I feel sick. I wouldn't mind a wash though.'

She looked and smelt like she hadn't had one in a few days.

'Why don't you go upstairs and have a shower or a bath then?' I suggested. 'You can have your old room back and I'll get your pyjamas out of the cupboard. Once you're clean I can look at the cuts on your feet and work out if I need to take you to hospital.'

'Hospital?' she gasped. 'I'm not going to any hospital. My parents might go there looking for me.'

'We'll see,' I said.

I knew Social Services would probably insist on me taking Shazia to A&E for a check-up to make sure she didn't have any internal injuries from her beating. I could see she was badly bruised, but she didn't seem to be in any pain. I didn't force the idea now though as I could see the idea of leaving my house was terrifying for Shazia.

★

When Shazia had gone upstairs, I gave myself five minutes to catch my breath before I picked up the phone. I needed this time to help me digest the information in my head before I could tell my fostering agency and Social Services the full story. I felt sick thinking about what she had told me. How could any parents do that to their own child and keep them prisoner like that?

I phoned my agency first. Because it was the early hours of a Saturday morning, it clicked through to the duty worker's mobile and I told her what had happened.

'She was brought here by her friend's mum and she's in a dreadful state,' I explained. 'She admitted that she was lying when she denied the story about being taken to Pakistan to get married and she's made some serious allegations about her parents. They've held her captive in the basement of their house for the last few days and she managed to escape by crawling out of the toilet window. I really do believe her when she says that she's in danger.'

The duty worker sounded as shocked as I had been.

'The poor girl,' she sighed. 'She must have been terrified.'

'She still is,' I told her. 'She said she fears for her life. If her own parents are capable of keeping her prisoner and starving her for days, then potentially they're capable of anything.

'What should I do?' I asked her. 'Am I OK to keep her here overnight?'

'I'll phone the duty social worker at Social Services straightaway, then I'll ring you straight back.'

Shazia was still in the bathroom when she called back twenty minutes later.

'I got through to Social Services, but unfortunately they're really stretched so I doubt whether a social worker will be able to get out to you tonight. They know Shazia is safe with you so they're happy for you to keep her overnight and then someone from the duty team will be in touch in the morning.

'Keep an eye on her,' she added. 'Obviously if you think she needs medical assistance or takes a turn for the worse, get her straight to hospital.'

'I will do,' I replied. 'She's battered and bruised but I don't think it's anything that can't wait until tomorrow. What about her parents? What will you tell them?'

'The local authority will get in touch with her parents tonight to let them know that Shazia is safe and that someone will be in touch with them in the morning.'

My gut feeling was that what Shazia needed most of all right now was sleep. Everything else could wait until the morning. After four days of constant anxiety and fear, she desperately needed to rest.

'Maggie, before I go, what other children have you got in the house right now?' the duty worker asked.

'My other placement, a toddler, is at his birth mum's having an overnight contact so it's just me and Shazia tonight,' I explained.

I knew she was doing a quick risk assessment.

'If at any point someone starts banging at the door or you're at all worried, please don't hesitate, just call the police,' she told me.

'I will,' I promised. 'I won't take any chances.'

'Is there anybody you can ask to come over tonight to be with you in case anything happens?' she asked.

'I don't know about coming over, but I've got a male friend I can ring who can be on standby in case I need him,' I said.

'That's probably a good idea,' replied the duty social worker. 'Hopefully you'll have a quiet night and you won't need to call on him.'

I hoped so too. I'd tried to reassure myself that Shazia's family wouldn't be able to find her here, but talking to the social worker had made me start to feel jumpy. I didn't think it was fair to call on Graham as I tried to keep our relationship separate from my fostering. My friend Vicky was a single carer too, but there was Anne and her husband Bob. Bob was a big burly bloke and he often helped me out with jobs around the house or if I had car trouble. Even though it was late, I decided to give him a call once Shazia was in bed.

Five minutes later, Shazia wandered downstairs with freshly washed hair and dressed in clean pyjamas.

'That's better,' I smiled. 'How are you feeling?'

She shrugged. 'Scared,' she sighed.

'Have you had much sleep over the past few days?'

She shook her head.

'It was horrible in that basement. All damp and cold and it smelt funny.'

Before she went to bed, I made her a cup of cocoa and a couple of slices of toast. While she ate, I had a quick look at her feet.

'You've got a few little cuts on your soles where you must have caught yourself when you were running so I'm going to stick a couple of plasters on them,' I told her.

I also got her to show me the burn on her arm.

'At least my mum bandaged it up for me,' she said sadly.

I gently lifted up the bandage. It was a nasty burn but thankfully it was clean and not infected so I put a new dressing on it.

'Come on, let's get you to bed,' I told her gently. 'Then we can talk some more in the morning. The local authority is happy for you to stay here tonight and a social worker will be in touch tomorrow.'

'But what's going to happen to me, Maggie?' she wondered, gazing up at me, suddenly looking much younger than her fourteen years.

'Don't worry about that now,' I told her gently. 'You need to try and get some sleep and then we'll work things out tomorrow. Social Services are going to tell your parents that you're safe so they won't be out looking for you.'

'Oh they will be,' Shazia sighed. 'I know my brothers. And they won't rest until they find me.'

I prayed for all our sakes that she was wrong.

EIGHT

Living in Fear

Walking into Shazia's room, I could see she was already tucked up in bed.

'Night, lovey,' I said.

'Where's Michael and Louisa?' she asked, the thought suddenly just coming into her head.

'Michael's sleeping at his mum's and Louisa's at Charlie's,' I explained. 'They got engaged last week so we had a little party for them tonight.'

The celebrations earlier this evening felt like a lifetime ago after everything that had happened in the past couple of hours.

'That's nice,' said Shazia, giving me a weak smile.

'You try and get some sleep now, lovey. I'll be downstairs if you need me.'

'I'll try,' she said bravely.

It wouldn't be long before I went to bed myself, but I needed some time to try and get my head around what had just happened. The adrenalin was still pumping through my veins after leaping into crisis mode and I didn't think I could switch off and go straight to sleep. Plus I knew I needed to phone my friend Anne. It was late and she had left the party hours ago so there was a good chance that she wouldn't even answer.

Much to my surprise, however, she did.

'Hello?' she asked as she picked up her mobile, a worried tone to her voice. 'Is everything alright, Maggie?'

'Anne, I'm so sorry to ring you at this time,' I told her.

'It's OK,' she said. 'Bob and I were just watching the end of a film. What's going on?'

'I've got a bit of a situation here tonight with one of the children I'm fostering,' I explained.

'Remember a few weeks ago I looked after a girl called Shazia?'

'Yes, I remember,' she said. 'I thought she'd gone. She wasn't at the party earlier, was she?'

'She had gone, but tonight after the party she came back and my agency are concerned in case her family turns up on my doorstep looking for her. It's very unlikely but if anything kicks off tonight, I wanted to ask if I could call on Bob to pop round if there's an emergency?'

'Of course you can, Maggie,' said Anne. 'We're only round the corner so he can be there in a few minutes. Do you want him to come over now?'

'No, honestly there's no need,' I reassured her. 'It's just good to know that if there is a problem, there's a big burly bloke on standby as well as the police. Thanks Anne.'

'It's not a problem,' she said. 'You look after yourselves and I hope you manage to get some sleep tonight.'

It reassured me to know that I could call on Bob, especially as he could probably get over here quicker than the police could if there was any trouble.

Five minutes after I'd spoken to Anne, my mobile rang. My heart sank when I saw Naz's number.

'What is it, Naz?' I asked her. 'What's happened?'

'Maggie, I wanted to warn you that Shazia's brothers have been round here,' she said hoarsely, her voice filled with panic.

'Oh no,' I gasped. 'When?'

'About half an hour ago,' she sighed. 'They were banging on the door but I wouldn't answer it, so they started shouting and swearing through the letterbox, demanding to know where Shazia was.'

'What did you tell them?' I asked.

'I didn't tell them anything,' she replied. 'I was terrified. My husband's out tonight so it's only me and Zeena in the house. I thought they were going to kick the door in so I called the police.'

She explained that thankfully the police had taken the threat seriously and had come round quickly.

'They asked the brothers why they were there and they said they were looking for their sister who had gone missing. When the police officers asked them if they wanted to fill in a missing person's report, they backed off and drove away.

'Afterwards the officers came in and spoke to me and I explained what had happened and said that Shazia was with you,' she continued. 'They said they would get in touch with Social Services just to clarify what I had told them and confirm that Shazia is safe.'

'No problem,' I said. 'That must have been so frightening, Naz. I'm sure the police will have scared them off, so hopefully they won't bother you again.'

As I put the phone down, a sense of unease crept over me. It was obvious that Shazia's brothers were determined to find her and they clearly weren't going to give up easily.

After I'd come off the phone to Naz, I crept upstairs to check on Shazia. There was no way I was going to tell her about her brothers turning up at Zeena's house. I knew that it would only add to her fears and make her feel even more threatened. At the end of the day, she was still only a child and she shouldn't have to deal with that.

She'd been in bed for twenty minutes and I was desperately hoping that she was fast asleep. But she was lying in the single bed, her eyes wide open.

'Maggie, I'm so tired, but I'm too scared to go to sleep,' she murmured. 'Every time I close my eyes I see my brothers coming for me. I don't want to be on my own. Please can I sleep with you in your room?'

'I'm sorry, lovey, but you can't,' I told her. 'It's against the rules for any child to sleep in my bedroom.'

The safeguarding policy for foster carers specified that I couldn't have a child in my bedroom. Kids could wander in and out, but they weren't allowed to sleep in my bed. It could be tricky sometimes, especially if I was looking after a toddler like Michael and they got poorly.

I could sit on the armchair in my bedroom and cuddle him, but I wasn't allowed to lie on my bed with him or let him sleep in my bed.

'Can you sleep in here with me instead?' she pleaded. 'You could have one of the bunk beds.'

'I'm not allowed to do that either,' I said apologetically. 'I'm really sorry, Shazia, but they're rules and I've got to follow them with every child.'

I did have another solution though.

'Grab your duvet and pillow and I'll make you a bed up on the sofa downstairs,' I told her. 'I'll sleep on the chair next to you. Does that sound OK?'

Shazia nodded eagerly and hurried to follow me downstairs.

My old, worn sofa was wide and squishy so it made quite a comfortable bed.

'Now you try and get some sleep,' I told her, stroking her hair. 'I'm going to lock up then I'll be right over here on this chair if you need anything. Shall I leave the lamp on in the corner?'

'Yes please,' she whispered. 'I don't want to be in the dark.'

Although common sense told me that there was no way Shazia's family knew where I lived or could trace her to here, I still felt slightly unnerved and on edge as I double-locked the front door. When I went into the kitchen to double-check the back door, I looked out of the window into the pitch black of the back garden.

Was there anyone out there in the darkness watching us?

A cold chill ran through my body and made me shudder. As I pulled down the kitchen blind, I prayed that we were in for a quiet night.

I triple-checked the front door was locked and the chain was on, then turned off the hallway light and crept back into the living room. Shazia shuffled around as I settled into the armchair and put a blanket over my legs. Unlike the sofa, the chair was hard and uncomfortable and I knew my chances of getting much sleep were minimal.

The same thoughts were going round and round in my mind.

Shazia's brothers were clearly on a mission to find her and I just prayed that their trail would run cold. If there was any trouble I knew I had Bob on standby, plus my house was in a row of terraces so if there was a kerfuffle on my doorstep, even in the middle of the night, I was sure one of my neighbours would hear and come to help.

After about twenty minutes I could tell Shazia was finally asleep. For the first time that evening since she'd arrived, I could see the muscles in her body had relaxed. Her sleep was very fitful, however. Over the next few hours she tossed and turned, crying out and mumbling to herself. God only knows what kind of dreams she was having.

I dozed on and off until it started to get light around five. Thankfully Shazia was still sleeping so I padded into the kitchen to make a cup of tea. My whole body ached from being curled up in a funny position on the chair, but I was filled with gratitude and relief that no one had turned up on the doorstep in the middle of the night.

As I flicked the kettle on, I stared out of the window at the bright summer's day just dawning. For some reason, I felt so much safer and less anxious now it was daylight. If Shazia's brothers knew where I lived, surely they would have turned up by now?

Just before 6 a.m. I heard Shazia calling me from the living room.

'Maggie? Maggie? Where are you?'

'It's OK, I'm here,' I called back, dashing in. 'I was in the kitchen having some toast.'

The look of fear and panic was back in her face.

'Did you sleep OK?' I asked her.

'Not really,' she sighed. 'I had a horrible dream. I was walking down your street and Adil jumped out of car with a knife. I was screaming and running for my life but it was too late. He got me on your doorstep.'

'Oh flower,' I soothed. 'That's not going to happen. You're safe here.'

'But how do you know?' she whispered, tears filling up her eyes.

'A duty social worker's going to call me this morning so we'll talk everything through with them,' I told her.

My mobile rang just as I was persuading a reluctant Shazia to eat some breakfast. It was a duty social worker that I knew called Maria. I walked upstairs to my bedroom so I could talk to her freely without Shazia overhearing.

'How are things this morning, Maggie?' she said.

'As you can imagine, we both had a restless night,' I told her. 'Shazia was tossing and turning and having bad dreams. But thankfully we've not heard anything from her family.'

'Good,' she said. 'Let's hope it stays that way.'

She explained that there was a note on the system to say the police had called them in the early hours of the morning to confirm that Shazia had been placed with me. I assumed that was to back up what Naz had told them.

'An officer will probably either call round or ring you today to double-check that and to speak to Shazia,' she said.

'That's fine,' I said. 'Obviously I won't open the door to anyone without seeing their ID.'

'How does Shazia seem in herself?' asked Maria.

'She's still very frightened, but that's understandable after everything she's been through over the past few days,' I said.

Maria explained that she'd sent an email to Rachel detailing everything and she would be in touch first thing on Monday to talk us through what needed to happen next.

'I imagine that she'll organise for the police to interview Shazia and possibly a medical check. Do you think she needs medical attention before then?' she asked.

'She's very weak, but she's eaten and I've made her drink lots of water,' I told her. 'She's awake and alert. She's got a burn on her arm that's pretty nasty, but it doesn't look infected. I put a clean dressing on it last night and I put some plasters on her feet where she's cut them. She's bruised, but she's told me that she's not in any pain, so my feeling is that any medical checks can wait until next week.'

'OK then,' replied Maria. 'Obviously keep in touch with us if you have any questions or concerns over the rest of the weekend. Otherwise Rachel will be in touch first thing on Monday.

'Oh, and Maggie – please don't send Shazia to school until you've talked everything through with Rachel.'

School was the last place I intended to send her as I knew that it would be the first place her brothers would know she might be.

'Can I have a chat to Shazia?' Maria asked.

'Yes, of course,' I said, taking the phone downstairs.

Shazia was sitting at the kitchen table, half-heartedly eating a bowl of cornflakes.

'The duty social worker Maria wants you to have a chat with her,' I explained.

She looked terrified as I passed her my mobile.

'Do I have to?' she whispered.

I nodded.

'She's not going to bite,' I smiled. 'She just needs to hear it from you that you're OK.'

Reluctantly Shazia said hello. I busied myself with putting away some clean dishes. All Shazia seemed to be saying was short, curt replies of 'Yes'.

'Yep, I'm fine being at Maggie's,' she said.

Then she passed the phone back to me.

'I know she's been through a lot, but that was like getting blood out of a stone,' sighed Maria. 'Anyway, she seems happy enough staying with you for the weekend so hopefully things will stay calm and Rachel will be in touch.'

'Thanks,' I told her.

After I'd put down the phone I tried to persuade Shazia to get dressed.

'It's a good job that you left a few clothes here from last time,' I told her.

Before she could reply, there was a knock at the door. We both stopped and looked at each other.

'I'll go and see who it is,' I whispered. 'You wait here.'

Poor Shazia looked as terrified as I felt as I slunk out into the hallway, praying whoever it was couldn't see me through the frosted glass of the front door. I crept into the front room and stared out through the nets of the bay window, desperately trying to make out who it was.

They knocked again, loudly and more urgently this time, and I almost jumped out of my skin.

Please don't let it be Shazia's brothers, I thought to myself.

Slowly and ever so slightly, I pulled the nets to one side to see two figures dressed in black on the doorstep. My stomach sank with relief as I saw the familiar uniform. It was two police officers.

'Coming,' I called as I ran to the front door.

I kept the chain on as I opened it, just to be safe, and the young female PC and her equally young male partner showed me their photo ID and introduced themselves.

'Come in,' I said, unlocking the door fully. 'Sorry, because of what's happened I'm having to be very careful.'

'No problem,' she smiled. 'We completely understand. Is Shazia Bains here? Can we speak to her please?'

'Yes, of course, come through,' I told them, showing them down the hall.

Shazia looked alarmed as the two officers walked into the kitchen.

'What is it?' she gasped. 'What's happened?'

'Nothing at all,' I told her, being careful not to mention anything about the events of the night before at Naz and Zeena's house. 'The officers are just here to check that you're OK.'

'Yes, I'm fine,' she said suspiciously.

'Our colleagues spoke to Social Services' duty team last night,' the female officer explained. 'But we needed to check for ourselves that you were here and you were safe.'

'I am safe here, but you're not going to tell my parents or my brothers where I am, are you?' gasped Shazia, her voice filled with panic. 'Then I definitely wouldn't be safe.'

'Don't worry, sweetheart,' the female officer soothed. 'We'll keep your whereabouts confidential. We just needed to clarify what your friend's mother had told us and make sure that you're OK.'

I could see by the uncertain look on Shazia's face that she wasn't sure whether to believe them.

I walked them back out to the hallway.

'As you can see, she's very jumpy and nervous,' I told them.

'I'm not surprised,' sighed the woman officer. 'From what her friend's mother said, she's been through a horrible ordeal. We'll need to speak to her about that in more detail.'

'Shazia's social worker is going to be in touch with us on Monday so she'll probably arrange for Shazia to be brought in for questioning then,' I told her.

'Whenever she's ready,' the officer smiled. 'I hope she's OK over the weekend. Do give us a ring if there are any problems.'

'Thanks officer, I will do,' I said, closing and locking the door behind them.

Shazia looked unnerved by the police visit.

'Come on, lovey, go and get yourself dressed,' I said, trying to inject a bit of normality back into the situation. 'Kerry will be dropping Michael back soon and at some stage Louisa will be back.'

I would have to tell Louisa the truth about what had happened as she lived in the house and the situation affected her too. But I decided that the fewer people who knew that Shazia was here, the better, so I wouldn't mention anything to Kerry just yet.

Thankfully the decision was taken out of my hands as Shazia was in the bathroom when Kerry arrived, so she didn't see her.

'How was the party last night?' Kerry asked.

'Oh it was lovely,' I said.

'And how's this little monkey been?' I added, picking up Michael and giving him a cuddle.

'Gorgeous,' she smiled. 'Although he wasn't as gorgeous when he woke up at five.'

'It's the light mornings,' I told her. 'I slept really badly last night too.'

'Yes, I was just thinking you looked tired,' she said. 'I hope you have a more restful night tonight.'

'So do I,' I sighed.

If she only knew the half of it.

After Kerry had said goodbye to Michael and left, I got some wooden blocks out for him in the kitchen.

When Shazia came down, dressed at last, he saw her and gave her a big grin.

'Michael!' she smiled, sitting down beside him on the floor and helping him build up the blocks.

It was a beautifully warm, sunny day, but I knew I couldn't risk any of us going outside.

Later that afternoon Louisa arrived back. I heard her letting herself in with her key and kicking off her boots in the hall. When she came into the front room and saw Shazia sitting on the sofa, she did a double-take.

'Hi Louisa,' Shazia smiled shyly.

'Er-hi,' Louisa replied, raising her eyebrows and giving me a look as if to say, 'What's happened now?'

She followed me through to the kitchen, leaving Shazia and Michael to watch TV.

'How come Shazia is back?' she asked in a low voice.

'It all kicked off last night after the party,' I explained, filling her in on the events of the night before.

'That's awful,' she sighed. 'The poor girl.'

'We've heard nothing from her family,' I told her. 'But I think we all need to be a little bit more cautious over the next few days.'

'Do you believe her, Maggie?' she asked.

'Yes,' I said at once. 'You should have seen the state that she turned up in. She was bruised, dirty and terrified. I could tell that her fear was very real. It still is.'

Last time Shazia had stayed with me, she had been eager to get out of the house at any opportunity, but now it was clear that she didn't want to leave the safety of these four walls. She didn't even want to be in a room on her own.

'It's very unlikely that her family knows this address or can trace me or her to this house, but we all have to be aware of the risk,' I told her. 'We need to be extra cautious about what we say to people and who we give this address to. Don't mention to anyone that Shazia's staying here and when you go out just keep an eye out that no one's hanging around outside or following you.'

'You're scaring me now,' said Louisa nervously.

I didn't want to worry her unnecessarily, but it was important that she understood the gravity of the situation in order to keep us all safe.

That night, I could tell that Shazia was still on edge.

'We all need to sleep upstairs in our own bedrooms tonight,' I told her.

There was no way I could face another night squashed up on that uncomfortable chair, but when I went up to check on her, the poor girl was still wide-awake and looking terrified.

'I've brought you a hot cocoa to help you feel sleepy,' I smiled, putting it down on the bedside table.

'Thank you,' she said meekly.

'I was going to go to bed and read, but would you feel better if I sat in here and read my book on the chair while you fall asleep?' I suggested.

She looked instantly relieved.

'Is that OK?' she asked. 'Do you mind?'

'No, that's fine,' I said.

I could see that she was exhausted and I understood that she was still a bundle of nerves and didn't want to be left on her own.

Thankfully, five minutes later she was in a deep sleep. I staggered off to bed, utterly exhausted, wondering what on earth tomorrow was going to bring.

NINE

Questions

The rest of the weekend passed with us all being very nervous and jumpy. Shazia was so scared that her brothers were out looking for her that thankfully she didn't question why she couldn't go out. None of us wanted to leave the safety of the house, even though the weather was hot and sunny. Everyone else in the country was sunbathing in gardens and parks, having barbecues and getting out their paddling pools, but we all stayed cooped up inside. The furthest I went was a quick trip to the supermarket on Sunday while Louisa stayed at home with Shazia and Michael.

Even though there wasn't any real risk if someone saw me on my own, I still felt myself looking nervously over my shoulder as I walked up and down the aisles. I got in and out of there as quickly as I could and breathed a sigh of relief as I walked through the front door with my bags of shopping.

'Everything OK?' asked Louisa.

I could see that she was feeling on edge too.

'Yes, fine,' I smiled, trying to muster up my most cheerful voice. 'No problem at all.'

Shazia was very quiet and I spent most of the weekend reassuring her.

'Rachel will come round tomorrow and talk us through everything,' I told her gently. 'You're safe here, Shazia. Nobody can find you.'

But I knew that none of us felt that convinced. Monday couldn't come soon enough as far as I was concerned.

Louisa had just gone off to work at eight-thirty when Rachel rang.

'Maggie, I've just seen my emails from the weekend,' she gasped as soon as I answered. 'I can't believe it. How's Shazia?'

'She's OK. Understandably she's still very frightened, but we had a quiet weekend and no one from her family has turned up, so hopefully she's starting to believe that she's safe here. Your instincts were right all along.'

'I wish they weren't,' she sighed. 'Poor girl. I can't believe they locked her up like that.'

Rachel explained that she was going to put a quick call in to the police as they had left her a message saying they wanted to speak to her about Shazia.

'As soon as I've done that, I'll pop round to see you both,' she said. 'Is that OK?'

'That's fine. I've got to drop Michael at Kerry's in the next half an hour but after that we're here for the rest of the day. Shazia doesn't want to leave the house at the moment.'

We'd been back ten minutes after dropping Michael when there was a knock at the front door. Shazia looked at me, her eyes filled with terror.

'It will probably be Rachel,' I reassured her.

But before I went into the hall, I peered out through the front window to check and only then opened the door to her.

'Hi Maggie,' she smiled.

Then she saw Shazia who had come out into the hallway.

'Shazia, how are you doing?' she asked, her eyes full of concern. 'What on earth has been happening?'

Shazia shrugged.

'Didn't Maggie tell you?' she said wearily.

'Yes, but I'd like to hear it from you as well,' Rachel replied.

'Why don't you two go into the front room and I'll put the kettle on?' I suggested.

By the time I'd made a pot of tea and come back in, Shazia had gone through everything with Rachel and I could see she was close to tears.

'I'm so sorry you had to go through this, Shazia,' Rachel told her. 'You must have been terrified. Why on earth didn't you say anything when I came round to your house?'

'I didn't know about the wedding then,' said Shazia. 'It was a few days later when I'd been measured for wedding clothes that I realised it was *my* wedding. After that they locked me up to stop me from telling anyone or getting help.'

I could see that Rachel still felt very guilty and responsible for what had happened, even though in reality there was nothing more we could have done.

'I spoke to the police this morning and they want to take a statement from you, Shazia,' she explained.

'No,' Shazia frowned. 'No way. I don't want to talk to the police. I don't want them speaking to my family.'

'Shazia, these are really serious allegations that you've made against your brothers and your parents,' I told her gently. 'The police need to check them out.'

'But what if the police tell them where I am?' she asked.

'They won't,' Rachel reassured her. 'This is a secure address and neither the police nor Social Services would ever disclose it to anyone in your family. We won't even tell them that you're at Maggie's.'

Despite Rachel's assurances, I was pretty sure that Shazia's family would assume that she was back in my care.

Rachel and I needed to have a chat alone, so while Shazia stayed in the front room and watched TV, we went into the kitchen.

'She seems very anxious,' sighed Rachel.

'She's not sleeping well,' I told her. 'To be honest, none of us are.'

'I'll talk to the police about security and then we'll need to have a meeting to work out where we go from here in terms of school and things like that,' she said.

'Are you going to go and talk to her parents?' I asked.

'Not until the police have,' Rachel replied.

In the meantime Social Services was going to apply to the court for an interim care order, which meant the local authority had overall parental responsibility for Shazia.

'While there's an ongoing police investigation, she won't have any contact with her parents,' Rachel told me.

'I don't think she'd want to,' I said. 'She's terrified of them finding her.'

Rachel explained that our main priority today was taking Shazia to be questioned by the police.

'Do we need to take her to the police station?' I asked.

Rachel shook her head.

'They said they'd take a statement from her at a safe house,' she replied.

It was a relief for me to hear that. From past experience when I'd been to pick up teenagers from there, the main police station in town was always noisy, with a crowded reception area full of drunks and dodgy characters. The interview rooms were bare and stark and the whole building was old and decrepit. It wasn't a place that I'd want to take a vulnerable, scared teenager.

'The police have given me the address so I'll drive us,' said Rachel. 'While she's there they also want a police doctor to check her over to see whether she needs hospital treatment for her injuries.'

'She seems OK,' I said. 'She's battered and bruised, but I've been keeping an eye on the burn on her arm and thankfully it seems to be healing.'

I knew we needed to take Shazia to the safe house as soon as possible as Michael was due back later on that afternoon.

'Do I have to go?' she sighed when we broke the news to her.

'Yes, lovey, it's really important that you talk to the police,' I told her. 'They want to keep you safe just like Social Services, and to do that they need to know what your family has done.'

Shazia looked like she was going to burst into tears as she reluctantly got into Rachel's car.

'It's going to be OK,' I said, desperately trying to reassure her. 'Rachel and I will be with you. You don't have to do this on your own.'

Half an hour later we pulled up outside a detached new-build house on a modern estate. I recognised it straightaway.

'I've been here before,' I told Rachel. Sadly I'd had several children in my care over the years who'd had to be interviewed and examined here.

'I think this is the one safe house for the whole area,' Rachel told me.

'Is this it?' asked Shazia nervously. 'It doesn't look like a police station.'

'Yes, sweetie,' I said. 'It's designed to look like an ordinary house so no one else knows it's here. The officers who work here are always very nice and kind and they're specially trained to deal with children.'

Shazia seemed slightly reassured, but she still hung back behind me as Rachel knocked on the front door.

A friendly-looking, grey-haired woman dressed in a shirt and trousers opened it.

'I'm DC Lorna Harris,' she said when Rachel and I had shown her our ID. 'Come on in.'

'And you must be Shazia,' she smiled.

'You don't look like a policeman,' Shazia said, looking her up and down warily.

'Well, they call us police officers these days,' DC Harris grinned. 'And I've been one for the past thirty years. Would you like a drink or something to eat before I show you around?'

Downstairs there was a living room and a kitchen.

'I've got a squash if you want one and there are plenty of crisps and biscuits if you're peckish,' she said, opening one of the cupboards.

'No thanks,' mumbled Shazia. 'I'm not hungry.'

As we were talking, a man came in. He had a baby face and like DC Harris, he wasn't in uniform.

'This is my colleague PC Rhodes,' said DC Harris.

He smiled at us.

'How about I give you a tour, Shazia?' he said. 'I'll take you to meet Dr Heslett, our police doctor, who's upstairs.'

She hung back reluctantly and glued herself to my side.

'Don't worry, we'll all come,' I reassured her.

'You've obviously seen the kitchen,' he said. 'That's a sort of living room in there but we use it more as an office. I'll show you upstairs to the interview rooms.'

On the way up the stairs we passed the huge bathroom that I also knew doubled as a medical examination room. Sadly I'd had to take a young rape victim in here a few years ago to be questioned and examined.

A blonde woman popped her head out of the bathroom. 'I'm Dr Heslett. Nice to meet you,' she said. 'I'll come and talk to you later, Shazia, after you've spoken to my colleagues.'

Upstairs at the front of the house were two big rooms.

'This is our interview room,' said PC Rhodes, taking us into one of them. There was a sofa in there and big plastic boxes full of toys. In each corner of the room there was a camera fixed to the wall.

'We have lots of toys and books here but I think you're a bit old for those,' he smiled.

'Yep, I don't play with toys any more,' sighed Shazia.

'Shazia, PC Rhodes and DC Harris are going to ask you some questions now,' Rachel explained to her.

'Questions about what?' she moaned. 'I've already told you what happened, and Maggie too.'

'You need to tell the police again,' I told her gently. 'It's really important they hear it from you. Rachel and I aren't allowed to be in the same room while you're being interviewed but we'll just be next door.'

Shazia looked nervously after us as we walked along the hallway and into the room opposite. She looked so vulnerable, and much younger than her fourteen years, and my heart went out to her. I'd also been in this room before and was familiar with the layout. There were a couple of chairs and a table with a large monitor on it. I switched it on and an image of the room next door flickered onto the screen.

Although Shazia had become distressed when she told me and then Rachel about what her family had done, she was almost in a trance as she told the police what had happened. How she had discovered her family was planning to take her to Pakistan, how her brother had held her arm over the hob and burnt it, then beaten her. How she was locked up for four days in the basement until she managed to escape through the bathroom window.

This time there were no tears. In fact she was almost devoid of any emotion.

'She's completely exhausted,' I sighed. 'Emotionally and physically.'

All I wanted to do was rush in there and take her home.

But Shazia's ordeal wasn't over yet.

'Before you go, Dr Heslett would like to check you over quickly and make sure that you don't need to go to hospital,' DC Harris told her, once they'd finished taking Shazia's statement.

'I'm fine,' Shazia insisted, looking alarmed at the thought of hospital.

'We just need to confirm that,' she smiled. 'After all, you were locked up for quite a long time.'

While Shazia was taken to the examination room, DC Harris took us downstairs for a chat.

'I wanted to warn you that these kinds of cases are incredibly difficult to prosecute,' she said. 'We're normally met with a wall of silence by the family and it's probably going to be Shazia's word against theirs.

'As you know, at present the forced marriage of a British citizen overseas isn't a criminal offence, although we hope that in the future this will change,' she continued. 'So the only possible charges that we could look at bringing would be assault and false imprisonment.'

'When will you be speaking to the family?' asked Rachel.

'We'll go round there today and hopefully question the parents and her brothers. I'll let you know how we get on.'

Half an hour later Shazia came downstairs with the police doctor. She looked shattered.

'Come on, Shazia, I'll take you into the kitchen for a packet of crisps while Maggie and Rachel have a chat with Dr Heslett,' said DC Harris.

'How did it go?' Rachel asked once Shazia and DC Harris were out of earshot.

'Shazia seems OK,' she nodded. 'As you said, her burn is healing nicely and she's bruised, but I don't think there's anything internal we need to worry about. I've taken some blood and urine so I will ring you when the results come back from the lab just in case anything concerning has shown up.'

'Thank you,' I told her.

On the drive back home Shazia hardly said a word. She didn't even want the packet of crisps the police had given her.

'Are you OK, lovey?' I asked.

'When can I go back to school again?' she said suddenly.

'Not yet,' Rachel told her. 'Me and Maggie and my managers need to have a meeting and work out how best to keep you safe. So you're definitely not going to be back for the next few days, I'm afraid.'

The next morning Rachel rang me.

'Hi Maggie,' she said. 'The police have just phoned. They spoke to Shazia's parents and brothers yesterday.'

'And?' I asked eagerly.

'Unfortunately, as they feared, it looks like a prosecution is going to be very unlikely.'

'How on earth did they explain holding her prisoner in the basement?' I sighed.

'They said Shazia was threatening to run away and they were trying to keep her safe. They pointed out that she had a history of making things up with Social Services. As we both know, it's not a crime to put a lock on a door.'

'What about the burn?' I asked, appalled.

'Her brother claimed she did that herself. That she held her hand on the hob.'

Even more frustratingly, the police had checked but this time there were no flights to Pakistan booked.

'I bet they were going to buy them at the last minute or even at the airport so they didn't arouse suspicion after last time,' I said.

'It's frustrating but the bottom line is, there's not a lot the police can do to warrant a prosecution sadly.'

It was exactly as the police had said – it would be Shazia's word against her family's.

'Shazia's going to be devastated,' I sighed. 'When will you tell her?'

'DC Harris and I will come round this afternoon.'

Dr Heslett also phoned me that morning.

'Shazia's test results have come back from the lab,' she said. 'She's slightly dehydrated so make sure she continues to have plenty of fluids. The other thing the tests showed is that she has a urine infection so I'll post you a prescription for some antibiotics for that. Apart from that, nothing else showed up in the bloods, but obviously keep an eye on her burn and check it's healing OK.'

'Thank you,' I said, relieved that it was nothing more serious. 'I will do.'

That afternoon, Rachel and DC Harris came round. Shazia looked alarmed when she saw them.

'It's nothing to worry about,' I told her. 'They just want to have a chat to you.'

'Will you stay with me, Maggie?' she asked, her eyes round with fear.

'Of course,' I said.

DC Harris had a very kind manner and I knew she would give her the news as gently as she could.

'Shazia, you were so brave when you told us what had happened to you at home,' she told her. 'I know it must have been hard for you and you did really well.

'Yesterday we went round and spoke to your parents and your brothers,' she continued.

'Did you?' gasped Shazia. 'What did they say?'

DC Harris explained how they'd denied all the allegations and said that she had made it all up.

'But that's not true,' sobbed Shazia. 'They're the ones who are lying, not me. I know I lied before but I'm not now. You've got to believe me.'

'We do believe you,' DC Harris assured her. 'We all believe you; we just don't think we have enough evidence to press charges against them.'

'I promise you I'm not lying,' Shazia cried, tears streaming down her cheeks.

She was inconsolable and it was heartbreaking to see her fear and frustration.

'So are you going to send me back home now?' she gulped. 'I can't go back. They'll kill me. You have to believe me – they'll kill me for bringing shame on the family again.'

She was hysterical.

'Shazia, we're not going to send you back home,' Rachel reassured her. 'At the moment you're going to remain in foster care while we work out what's best for you in the long term. I need to talk to my managers and work out where we go from here. But we do believe you and we will take your wishes into consideration.'

'Even though we can't prosecute your parents for any crime, we're taking this very seriously and we'll do all we can to help Social Services keep you safe,' DC Harris added.

She explained how they had 'red kited' my address, which meant that if there was a problem and I called 999, I could give them a special codeword and they would put me straight through to someone who knew about our situation and could get help there ASAP.

'Your codeword is Operation Taco,' DC Harris told me.

'That sounds funny,' said Shazia, wiping her tears away with her sleeve.

'We just pick random peculiar words so you're more likely to remember them,' smiled DC Harris.

I hoped it would help Shazia feel a little bit safer.

That night my phone rang and Graham's number flashed up on my screen.

'Hi Maggie, I was just ringing to check you were still in the land of the living as I haven't heard from you for a few days,' he joked.

'I also wondered if you fancied a walk and a pub lunch one day next week?'

'I'm sorry,' I told him. 'I'd love that but Shazia's come back so I've been concentrating on her for the last few days and I've still got my hands full. I'm afraid I can't really say much more than that.'

'Don't worry,' he replied. 'I know you can't tell me much. So I'll assume our daytime dates are over for the time being?' he asked, sounding a little disappointed.

'Yes, I'm afraid so. It's a bit tricky to leave the house at the moment if I'm honest. But hopefully things will calm down.'

Thankfully, Graham had been seeing me long enough to know that I liked to keep him separate from my fostering. He knew that because of confidentiality I couldn't tell him much about specific children but nevertheless, I knew it frustrated him that we couldn't see more of each other. I missed him but, as ever, I was grateful that he was so understanding.

I really did hope what I'd told him was true and things would start to calm down. After a stressful few days, I was ready for a bit of peace and quiet. However, things never work to plan.

TEN

House Arrest

The next big issue that we had to address was school. Shazia was desperate to go back to her old school but the question was, would she be safe there? After all, it was the one place where her family knew they could find her.

She'd been off for three days when Rachel and I had a conversation about it.

'Even though Shazia's terrified of her family getting to her, she's adamant about going back to her old school,' I told her.

'I can understand why,' said Rachel. 'It would be less disruptive to her education if she stayed at the same school. Plus it's the summer term and there's only around six weeks of school left.'

'And Zeena and her friends are all there,' I pointed out.

I knew how important friendships were for teenage girls and school was the only familiar thing left in Shazia's life.

'Let's organise a meeting with the Head and see if there's any way we can work something out to help manage the risk,' said Rachel.

The following day Rachel and I went for a meeting with Mrs White, the head teacher at Shazia's school. Michael wasn't seeing Kerry that day so I arranged for him and Shazia to go to Vicky's. But Shazia wasn't best pleased that I was leaving her there.

'I'm not a baby,' she moaned. 'I don't need babysitting.

'Why can't I stay at your house?'

'Because after everything that's happened, I don't want to risk leaving you on your own,' I explained. 'What if your brothers turned up on my doorstep looking for you?'

'OK,' she sighed. She didn't look happy about it, but at least she understood why I was insisting that she went to Vicky's.

I had already met Mrs White from when Shazia had been taken into care the first time around. She was waiting for us at the reception.

'I was so shocked to hear what had happened,' she said, as she walked us down the corridor to her office. 'We knew Shazia had been off sick for a few days but we had no reason to question it. How's she doing?'

'She's OK,' replied Rachel. 'She desperately wants to come back to school and I think it would do her good to have some normality and routine back. But after everything that's happened with her family and the allegations she's made against them, we really need to know that if she comes back, she's going to be safe.'

'Of course,' Mrs White nodded.

Between us we came up with some basic rules.

'It makes sense that Shazia has to stay on the school grounds at all times,' said Rachel.

'Even at lunchtime?' asked Mrs White. 'A lot of the pupils go to the local shops.'

Rachel shook her head.

'She'll have to stay on school grounds,' she replied firmly. 'We could do with one main contact at school who takes responsibility for knowing where Shazia is at any given time.'

'I'm sure her form teacher, Mrs Roebuck, wouldn't mind doing that,' said Mrs White. 'I know Shazia gets on well with her. What about getting her to and from school?'

'I'll drive her to school every day and pick her up,' I told her. It would be a hassle but I was prepared to do it.

'Rather than just dropping her off, Maggie, are you OK to walk her into the building and hand-deliver her to her classroom?' asked Rachel.

'Yes, of course,' I nodded. 'In the afternoon I'll come into the school building as well and pick her up from the classroom.'

'We should be able to sort you out a space in the staff car park to make it more secure,' said Mrs White.

'Obviously if anyone turns up or rings in asking for information about Shazia, please direct them straight to Social Services and don't confirm whether she's in school or not,' Rachel told her. 'The only people who will ever contact you about Shazia are myself and Maggie.'

'Of course,' said Mrs White. 'I'll make sure the office staff are fully briefed.'

'Even though the police don't feel they have enough evidence to lead to a prosecution, we feel that Shazia's family pose a significant risk to her safety and both Social Services and the police are taking it very seriously,' Rachel told Mrs White. 'I'm sure you've read cases about honour killings where young women have been murdered because they refused to be forced into a marriage by their families.'

'Sadly I have,' sighed Mrs White.

'After the threats that Shazia's brother Adil has made, we don't want to take the risk,' Rachel explained.

It was a sobering thought for all of us and it brought home how real the threat was to Shazia.

It was decided that she would start back at school on Monday of the following week.

After the meeting, Rachel and I walked out into the car park together.

'Well, that went OK,' she said. 'At least the school is prepared to work with us.'

'I'll go back and give Shazia the good news,' I replied.

On the drive home from Vicky's, Shazia was sat in the front seat next to me while Michael was babbling away in his car seat in the back. I told her how the meeting had gone and what was discussed.

'The good news is, we've worked out a way for you to go back to school so you can start next week,' I told her.

I expected her to be pleased, but she didn't seem happy with the arrangements that we'd put in place.

'You have to drop me off and pick me up from my teacher?' she moaned. 'It's worse than primary school. And I can't even go to the shops with Zeena at lunchtime?'

I shook my head.

'You can't leave the school premises I'm afraid,' I said. 'We're not doing this for fun, lovey. Your brothers know you're at that school and they probably know you go out at lunchtime to the shops with the rest of the pupils so it's an easy way for them to get to you.

'The school can't protect you when you're not on school grounds. Do you really want to take that risk?'

I could see that it had finally dawned on Shazia and she shook her head.

'If you want to go back to your old school, this is the way it's got to be,' I said firmly.

Over the past few days since Shazia had come back into my care, I'd been in constant touch with my supervising social worker Becky. When I got home I rang to fill her in about what was happening with Shazia's school.

'While I've got you, Maggie, I'm afraid I need to do a risk assessment,' she said.

I knew it was procedure, but my heart sank at the mention of those two words.

'I need to judge if Michael is at risk by being in the same placement as Shazia when all this is going on,' she added.

The worst-case scenario was that if Becky deemed it unsafe for Michael and Shazia to be in the house together, I would have to choose between the two of them. One of them could stay and the other child would have to go.

'Please don't make me choose,' I begged. 'You know I've had to make decisions like that before and it's always horrendous.'

'Hopefully it won't come to that, Maggie,' she told me.

We talked about how now that contact had increased, Michael was spending most weekdays at his mum's house.

'How's Kerry coping?' Becky asked.

'Really well,' I smiled. 'She loves having him with her and he's doing a couple of overnights a week now. To be honest, he's hardly here any more.'

'I'm waiting to hear back from Helen, his social worker, but I expect that in the next few weeks we'll start the handover and he'll go back to Kerry full time.'

I knew Helen wanted to do things as gently as possible to check that Kerry felt she could cope. The gradual process was also helping to ease me into it and I was slowly getting used to not having Michael around all the time.

'Well, my feeling is because Michael isn't with you that much now I don't believe he's at risk,' Becky told me. 'Particularly as in all likelihood he won't be there much longer.'

It was such a relief to hear that. Kerry had noticed that Shazia was back living with me but I hadn't told her anything about why and she hadn't asked. Understandably, she was so caught up with Michael and her own mental health issues that any other placements I had weren't really at the forefront of her mind.

Keeping Shazia safe also affected what we did at home. It meant that we had to think carefully about where we went and what we did. We couldn't go shopping into the town centre, for example, or to the big retail park or the cinema on the outskirts of town as we couldn't risk any of Shazia's family seeing us together or following us home. We couldn't even go for a walk in the park. I talked everything through with Rachel beforehand, as I didn't want to take any unnecessary risks.

'Either stay very local or go as far out of the area of possible,' she advised me.

So when I needed to get Shazia some new clothes and shoes, we had to go shopping in a city nearly two hours' drive away. It was hard work having to think everything through before I did it, but I had dealt with these kinds of situations before. In the past I'd fostered several children whose parents had threatened to snatch them so I'd had to be constantly on my guard. I'd even once gone as far as dressing a baby boy as a baby girl to avoid detection when I wanted to go out.

I never let my guard down and even in the house I was very jumpy. I wouldn't answer the door to anyone I wasn't expecting and I didn't answer my phone if it was a number that I didn't recognise. Whenever I drove anywhere I always looked around to make sure no one was following us. I couldn't risk Shazia going out on her own but I could tell she was going stir-crazy being cooped up in the house all the time and having me with her constantly.

'Do you think her friend Zeena could come round here at the weekend?' I asked Rachel. 'It would really cheer Shazia up.'

It was a risk as Shazia's family knew Zeena's address, but Rachel and I talked it through carefully ahead of time. We planned it like a military operation and got Naz's permission, then we organised for a taxi to pick Zeena up rather than Naz or I taking her. It dropped her off a couple of streets away and Louisa went out to meet her and walked her back to our house as Shazia's family didn't know her. Even then, just to make sure, she brought her through the back entrance in the garden.

All of the careful planning was worth it when I saw the look on Shazia's face when Zeena walked into the kitchen.

'I told you I had a surprise for you,' I smiled.

'Zee!' she beamed, her eyes wide with delight and the two girls fell into a hug.

It was the first time I'd seen a genuine smile from her since she'd come back to my house.

Zeena spent the day with us. The girls understood they couldn't go out, even though it was another blisteringly hot day, but they watched a DVD and had pizza.

Halfway through the film, Shazia came storming angrily into the kitchen.

'Why didn't you tell me, Maggie?'

'Tell you what?' I asked, puzzled.

'That my brothers had been to Zeena's house looking for me? She told me how her and her mum had to call the police when they were banging on the door.'

'That was the first night that you came here and you were scared stiff,' I sighed. 'You were so traumatised after everything that had happened and you couldn't sleep. I didn't want to worry you even more. I was doing it to protect you.'

Unfortunately Shazia didn't see my reasoning.

'You should have told me,' she sighed. 'You see, I told you they'd be out looking for me.'

'Well hopefully they've got the message now and have realised they won't find you,' I told her.

'I wish. Zee says she sees my brother Adil all the time. He drives past the end of her street when she's walking home from school.'

It was the first I'd heard about this and I was unnerved by the fact that Shazia's brothers were still trying so hard to find her. I went into the living room to speak to Zeena.

'Does Adil say anything to you when you see him?' I asked her.

She shook her head.

'He just slows the car down and watches me but I just stare him out.'

'Have you told your mum or the police this?' I asked.

'Nah,' shrugged Zeena. 'It would just freak her out and Adil hasn't done anything. He's just a creep.'

She might have dismissed it but I knew I had to pass this information on to Social Services.

'You see, Maggie?' said Shazia looking nervous. 'I told you he wouldn't give up. It's never going to be over. They're not going to stop until they've found me.'

For once, I feared that she was right.

Now that the police had finished their investigation, Rachel was able to go round and talk to Shazia's family about everything and hear their side of things. I was intrigued to hear what they were going to say and she came round to see me straight afterwards.

'It was as exactly as the police found,' she sighed. 'They're blaming Shazia for everything. They said she was threatening to run away – that's why they turned the basement into her bedroom. Apparently she burnt her own arm and was telling lies again about being forced to get married in Pakistan.'

I shook my head.

'I told them that we hadn't made a decision yet about Shazia's long-term future, but at this point in time she was saying that she didn't want to go back.'

'How did they take that?' I asked.

'Mum was quiet, Dad was furious,' she said. 'He was ranting and raving saying what does she know. He said that she's a child and they're her parents so they know best. I tried to explain to him that Social Services has to listen to a young person's wishes and this was what Shazia was telling us.'

Rachel was completely right. When deciding on an older child's future, Social Services had to take into account what that child wanted. You couldn't make a young person of Shazia's age return home if they didn't want to.

'They asked me if they could they see her, but I told them in no uncertain terms that when there's a question about a child's safety, I couldn't allow them to have access,' Rachel added.

'Her dad and brothers were clearly furious and they kept talking to each other in Punjabi. On my way out, Shazia's brother Adil cornered me.'.

'He's the one who gave me a hard time at her first contact session,' I replied.

'He was very aggressive,' she said. 'He told me not to worry, that they'd find Shazia and bring her home.'

A cold shiver ran through me.

'What did you say?' I asked.

'I asked if he was threatening her and he said no and walked off.'

Hearing what had happened at Shazia's parents' house only made me more certain that foster care was the right place for Shazia to be.

'Despite what her family is saying, I believe Shazia,' I told Rachel. 'I can see how scared she is of them. I can normally tell when kids are lying. Real, genuine fear isn't something you can make up or turn on and off when you feel like it. She is terrified of what her own family is capable of.'

'I agree with you,' Rachel nodded. 'It's clear that something has gone on. She was battered and bruised when she turned up here and we can't ignore the burn on her arm.'

It was clear that there was no way we could send Shazia home.

'While we work out a long-term solution, are you OK for Shazia to continue to stay with you?' Rachel asked.

I didn't even need to think about it.

'Of course I am,' I said. 'She's lost her entire family. We're all she has right now. I think she's starting to feel safe here and it would disrupt everything again if we moved her to another carer.'

'You do know this is going to put a lot of restrictions on where you can go and what you can do, Maggie,' Rachel told me.

'I know,' I said, 'but we're coping and I'm willing to do that for Shazia.'

In a way, I felt like I owed it to her to make this sacrifice. She had come to me for help and I didn't want to let her down.

The whole thing was really unsettling. It was clear that Shazia's family was intent on finding her and they weren't willing to give up without a fight.

ELEVEN

A Lucky Escape

Glancing in my rearview mirror, I realised the silver Toyota was still behind me.

I could feel the panic rising in my throat.

Don't be silly, Maggie, I told myself. The car's not following you, you're being paranoid.

But for the past twenty minutes, since I'd dropped Shazia at school, every turn I had taken from the minute I'd come out of the car park, that car had taken it too. I couldn't make out the driver because of the bright sunlight, but I was convinced it was a member of Shazia's family.

OK, I would test them again.

Suddenly, without stopping to indicate, I turned left. I looked in my mirror and realised with horror that the Toyota was still there looming behind me.

I was getting more and more uneasy now, and I felt like I was in some TV police drama.

But this was no drama. This was real life and I was getting closer to my street. If it was Shazia's family following me, there was no way I was going to pull up outside my house and lead them straight to where I lived.

Think, Maggie, think, I willed myself, the panic rising in my chest.

Taking a sharp turn, I quickly pulled into a side street and stopped. I breathed a sigh of relief as the silver car drove straight on. As it passed I turned and caught a glimpse of the driver – a young blonde woman in her twenties who probably had nothing to do with either Shazia or her family.

I felt my shoulders relax and I rested my head on the steering wheel. It was only then I realised my hands were shaking.

'Pull yourself together, Maggie,' I told myself aloud. 'Stop being so paranoid.'

I looked in my rearview mirror and saw Michael grinning at me from the back seat.

'Are you OK back there, cheeky face?' I smiled at him. 'Don't mind me, I'm just losing the plot here.'

Shazia had started back at school three days ago and, much to everyone's relief, things were going well. She had settled back in OK and although we were both on tenterhooks at first, everything had gone smoothly. It was clear that all the extra security measures we'd put in place had made Shazia feel calmer and less paranoid, and she was enjoying being back into a routine and seeing her friends.

But while Shazia might have relaxed a little, as this morning had shown, I was still on high alert. Whenever I left the school car park, I looked in my mirror to check no one was following me. I did the same when I picked Shazia up. I couldn't relax and I was constantly looking over my shoulder.

*

I took a few deep breaths to calm myself down before I got back on the road. After the incident with the silver car, I was running late now so I dropped Michael straight to Kerry's for the day and then headed home to catch up on some cleaning. I'd arranged to meet Graham later that day for lunch. In the ten days since Shazia had been back, I had hardly left the house apart from meetings with Social Services and the odd rushed trip to the shops, so I was going to take advantage of the fact that she was at school and I could go out and about in public again. I'd arranged to meet him at a local café.

'Hello stranger,' he grinned as I walked in.

'Hi,' I smiled back, bending down and giving him a kiss. 'It's so nice to see you. I'm sorry about the past week or so. I've been under house arrest because of what's been going on at home.'

'It's OK,' he said. 'You don't have to explain.'

Thankfully Graham understood that I had to keep details of my fostering work confidential so he never pushed me to tell him anything. The fact that he was someone who was completely separate from my fostering meant that I could fully switch off when I was with him and it was a relief to have a break after the constant anxiety of the last few days.

I really had missed him and we had so much to talk about that at first, I didn't hear my mobile ringing in my bag. By the time I felt the vibration against my leg and had reached for it, it had gone to voicemail. My stomach lurched when I saw who the missed call was from.

Shazia's school.

'Sorry Graham, I need to listen to this message,' I told him. 'It might be something urgent.'

I struggled to hear the voicemail above the hustle and bustle of the busy café. The background music, the whir of the coffee machine and a baby crying on the next table meant I couldn't work out who it was or what they were saying.

'I'm just going to pop outside,' I told him, panicking now. 'I can't hear a thing in here.'

Finally, stood out on the pavement, I pressed my ear against the phone and heard Mrs White's well-spoken voice.

Why on earth was Shazia's head teacher ringing me?

'Maggie, it's Anna White. There's been a bit of an incident with Shazia. Please can you come up to school as soon as you can? It's urgent. Thanks.'

My hands were shaking as I hung up and ran back into the café.

'I'm so sorry, Graham, I have to go,' I said, grabbing my bag off the floor.

'What, right now?' he sighed. 'You haven't even finished your sandwich.'

'I'm really sorry, but I have to,' I said apologetically, giving him a quick hug.

I bolted out of the café and back to my car. As I hurried down the high street, I tried to ring the school back but it kept clicking on to the office answer machine.

I looked at my watch.

12.50 p.m. Most of the staff would probably be on their lunch break now.

Rather than waste more time on trying to call, I decided to jump straight in the car and drive up there as quickly as

I could. So many scenarios were running through my mind. Had Shazia done something terrible? I didn't think that was likely as she was generally a well-behaved pupil. Had she had an accident and been hurt? Or my worse-case scenario, had something happened with her family? Had they somehow managed to sneak into school and get to her?

A knot of nerves twisted in my stomach as I pulled into the school car park. I grabbed my bag and ran to the office in the main reception.

'I'm Shazia Bains' foster carer, Maggie Hartley,' I gasped breathlessly to the middle-aged woman behind the desk. 'Mrs White called me and said there'd been some sort of incident.'

'Oh yes,' she said, a concerned look on her face. 'They're in one of the Year Nine classrooms. I can show you where.'

'It's OK,' I interrupted. 'I know where I'm going.'

The Year Nine block was where I dropped off and picked up Shazia every day. I ran down the corridor, glancing into classrooms as I went by. Lunch time must have just finished and they were all full of children doing lessons until I got to the last one. Through the glass I could see Mrs White, Zeena and – my heart sank with relief – Shazia, all sitting on plastic chairs.

I was so relieved to see her; I didn't even knock and barged straight in.

'Shazia!' I gasped. 'What on earth has happened?'

Her white school shirt was all ripped and her face was streaked with tears. Zeena was sat next to her and she looked just as dishevelled. Both girls looked completely shell-shocked and didn't say a word.

'Ah, Maggie, thanks for coming so quickly,' said Mrs White, her expression grim.

'Is someone going to tell me what's been going on?' I demanded.

Shazia looked at Zeena. I could see her whole body was shaking.

'I'll go and get you a drink of water while you talk to Maggie,' Mrs White told her gently.

'Shazia, please talk to me,' I repeated. 'What's happened?'

'It was my brothers,' she gulped. 'They tried to snatch me. They tried to pull me into a car.'

I was so shocked that I could hardly take in what she was telling me.

'Your brothers?' I gasped. 'But how could they do that? How on earth did they get into the school?'

'We weren't at school,' she mumbled sheepishly. 'We went to the shops at lunchtime and they were waiting there.'

'You did what?' I exclaimed.

I could see Shazia was upset and shaken, but I couldn't stop the anger rising up inside me. I was furious with her for putting herself at risk like that.

'Shazia, after everything that we talked about, everything you've said to me about being terrified of your brothers finding you, what on earth were you thinking?' I raged.

'I just fancied some chips from the chippy,' she said meekly, looking at the floor. 'Nothing's happened since I've been back and it was so boring staying in the building every day.

'I'm sorry,' she sobbed. 'I thought it was going to be OK.'

Zeena leant over to her and put her arm around her friend.

'Sorry Maggie,' she sighed. 'It was only across the road. We didn't think it would matter.'

I couldn't believe what I was hearing. Shazia was prepared to risk her own safety and for what? A bag of chips.

I took a deep breath to try and calm myself down. I needed to know what had gone on so that I could call Rachel and potentially the police.

'Start from the beginning and me exactly what happened,' I told her.

Mrs White came back in with a glass of water and handed it to Shazia. She gulped it down.

'It was boiling hot outside and I was fed up of being stuck in school on my own every lunchtime so I thought I'd nip to the chippy with Zee,' she said. 'It's only across the road and I knew we'd be there and back in five minutes. I didn't think anyone would ever know or notice we'd gone.'

'Where was Mrs Roebuck?' I asked.

'Unfortunately she was in a meeting that overran,' said Mrs White apologetically. 'As soon as she came out she went to check on Shazia in the classroom but she wasn't there so she went to look for her in the canteen.'

'It wasn't her fault,' sighed Zeena. 'We snuck out to go to the chippy.'

'We were walking back to school with our chips,' said Shazia, swallowing a lump in her throat. 'I didn't even notice the car parked up there on the street.

'It wasn't even Adil's car. I didn't know they were outside school waiting.'

I shuddered at the thought of the girls walking straight into their trap.

'As we was walking past, the passenger door flew right open,' she sobbed. 'It made me jump and I didn't realise what was happening. Then someone tried to pull me into the car,' she sobbed. 'When I looked up I realised it was my brother Dev. Adil was in the driver's seat. I was kicking and screaming and lashing out and calling for someone to help me. He was shouting and swearing at me, telling me to shut up and get in the car. But I didn't want to, Maggie.'

She struggled to continue, her voice shaking with emotion.

'I kicked him and scratched his face and he ripped my shirt. 'Then Adil leaned across to help him and I thought that was it. That they'd got me.'

I couldn't even imagine how scared she must have been and I felt a rush of anger towards her brothers.

'Zee was epic,' she said, giving her a weak smile. 'She was screaming and screaming for help and some people ran out of the chip shop. Dev got out to try and force me into the car but Zee kicked him.'

'Right in the privates,' Zeena said proudly. 'Then I threw my can of Coke in his face.'

Shazia described how she'd managed to wrestle free in the commotion and the two girls had run into the chip shop for safety.

'What did your brothers do?' I asked.

'As soon as they saw we were in the shop with the manager, they drove off,' she said.

'Poor Shaz was just shaking and shaking,' sighed Zeena. 'She was so scared after what they said to her.'

I looked at Shazia.

'What did they say?' I asked her.

'Adil told me that it didn't matter how long I ran from them, they'd get me in the end,' she whispered, her eyes filled with pure fear. 'He said they would never give up and that next time. . .'

Her voice trailed off as she started to cry.

'Next time what, lovey?' I asked gently.

'Next time he was going to kill me,' she sobbed.

I wrapped my arms around her, stroking her dark hair.

'Oh Shazia, that's horrible,' I soothed. 'You must have been so frightened.'

She nodded, wiping away her tears.

I could see she was upset but I also couldn't help feeling really cross with her. What was the point of us putting all these security measures in place if she was going to do something silly like this?

'I'm sorry, Maggie,' she said, tears streaming down her face. 'I'm so sorry.'

After everything that had happened, I knew I had to get Shazia away from school and back to my house as quickly as possible. Then I needed to call Rachel.

'Take care, Maggie,' said Mrs White as I helped Shazia get her things together. 'I hope Shazia's OK. Zeena's mum is on the way to pick her up too.'

'Tell her I'll probably give her a ring later,' I replied. 'I'm going to call Rachel the social worker as soon as I get back and we'll be in touch.'

The two girls gave each other a hug.

'Bye Shaz,' sighed Zeena. 'I hope you're OK.'

'Thanks for helping me,' she said. 'Love you, Zee.'

We walked back to the car in silence, Shazia looking stunned and exhausted after the afternoon's events. I felt for her but I was still furious about what she'd done.

Shazia was quiet the whole journey back.

'What's going to happen now?' she asked quietly as we pulled up outside the house.

'I don't honestly know,' I sighed. 'I'm going to call Rachel now and tell her what's happened. We'll have to have a meeting and decide where we go from here.'

Shazia nodded. She looked terrified.

As soon as we got in, Shazia went up to her room and I went into the kitchen and called Rachel. She was as incredulous as I had been about what the girls had done.

'She did what?' she gasped as I'd told her what had happened.

'She's very shaken up and scared but to be honest, she's lucky that she managed to get away,' I told her. 'It was a really close call.'

'I'll come round now and have a chat,' she said.

I could see Shazia was scared about seeing Rachel when she came downstairs.

'Have you told her what I did?' she asked, fiddling with her school skirt.

'Of course I have,' I replied. 'She needs to know the full story.'

Rachel was far calmer than I had been when she came round, but it was clear that she was as frustrated with Shazia as I was.

'Shazia, I'm so disappointed in you,' she said. 'You put yourself at risk. You're lucky things didn't turn out a lot worse. You could be halfway to Pakistan by now and there would be nothing that we could do to help you.'

'I'm sorry,' Shazia mumbled meekly.

'What's going to happen now?' she asked. 'Can I go back to school?'

'I honestly don't think you can,' sighed Rachel. 'Your safety's at risk and I don't think we've got any option other than to remove you. How do we know you're not going to do this again?'

'But I promise I won't,' said Shazia, her eyes filling with tears again. 'I'll do anything you want.'

'Shazia, it's too much of a risk. Your brothers have clearly been waiting outside the school and watching you. Who's to say they're not going to follow Maggie home one afternoon or manage to get into the school building the next time? That not only puts you at risk but Maggie and potentially Michael too.'

'But even if I don't go to school, can I still see Zeena?' she asked.

Rachel shook her head.

'I don't think it's a good idea at the moment,' she said. 'We know that your brothers know where she lives.'

'But what about getting her a taxi round like we did before?'

'After what happened today, I don't think we can take the risk again,' Rachel told her. 'I'm sorry, Shazia. We're not doing this to be mean. Social Services' job is to keep you safe and today proved that your brothers are still a very real threat. 'They're not going to give up.'

This was the final nail in the coffin for Shazia and she dissolved into tears.

'It's so unfair,' she sobbed, storming out of the kitchen and stomping upstairs.

'I'll talk to her later,' I told Rachel.

We needed five minutes just to have a private word on our own and I knew Kerry was due to drop Michael off at any moment.

We sat down at the kitchen table together.

'Perhaps I was naïve letting her go back to school in the first place?' Rachel sighed.

'We had to give it a go, and there was no knowing that things would turn out like this,' I replied.

'I'm going to have to talk to my manager about this and work out what we do next,' she added. 'In the short term, home schooling until the summer holidays is probably the only option. But we need to start thinking what's best for Shazia in the long term.

'I'm going to ring DC Harris now and see if there's anything they can do from a police point of view,' she continued. 'And depending on what they say, I'll go round and talk to Shazia's family and explain that they're not allowed to approach or threaten her like that.'

'Good luck,' I said. 'I think you're going to need it.'

From my experience of Shazia's brothers, I knew they could be very menacing. On my one meeting with him when we'd bumped into Adil in the car park on the way to contact, he'd made the hairs on the back of my neck stand up.

After Rachel had gone I went up to see Shazia in her room. She was very teary and I could see that the drama at lunchtime had exhausted her.

I sat on the bed with her and stroked her hair.

'I'm going to miss Zee so much,' she sobbed.

'Perhaps in time you might be allowed to ring her and maybe see her, just not right now,' I told her gently. 'Your brothers know Zeena is your best friend, and after what happened today they might target her. 'I'm sure you could write to her and Rachel will pass the letters on.'

I managed to persuade her to come down and eat something. But when Louisa walked in the door after work she burst into tears again.

'What's happened?' Louisa asked, stunned, looking at me.

'Poor Shazia's had a horrendous day,' I explained. 'Her brothers tried to drag her into a car at the shops outside school today but thankfully she managed to get away.'

'Oh God,' gasped Louisa. 'You poor thing. That must have been so frightening.' She looked confused. 'But why were you at the shops? I thought you weren't allowed out of school?'

'I only wanted to get some chips with Zeena,' babbled Shazia. 'I didn't know they were waiting for me. It's not fair. I just want to be normal like everyone else.'

'I know you do,' said Louisa, giving her a hug. 'But you're too important to risk. Everyone just wants to keep you safe, Shazia, so you've got to listen to them and do what they tell you.'

It was helpful having someone closer to Shazia's age talking it through with her.

Shazia was still very teary and upset and I understood why. Everything in her life had gone – her family, her friends and now her school. It was all starting to hit home that life was never ever going to be the same for her again.

TWELVE

Moving On

Later on that evening, Zeena's mum Naz called.

'I heard what happened at school today,' she sighed. 'Zeena's very shaken up and to be honest, so am I.'

'How's Shazia doing?' she asked. 'She must have been terrified.'

'She's OK but I don't think we can risk her going back to school again,' I told her.

'I thought that might be the case,' replied Naz. 'To be honest. Maggie, I'm relieved. I care about Shazia, I really do, and I know the girls are best friends, but my main concern is my daughter's safety. As long as Zeena's hanging around with Shazia I feel that she's at risk. I don't want her family turning up here again or her brothers threatening her or us.'

'I understand,' I said. 'I agree that it's best the girls don't see each other for a while. Shazia's very upset about it, but I've explained that it's just for the next few weeks, then hopefully after that, things will have settled down and we can reassess the situation.'

'Zee will miss Shazia too,' she sighed. 'I'm dreading telling her they can't see each other but hopefully she'll understand.'

Even though Shazia did understand our reasoning, she was still fed up about not being able to go to school. The school was going to email her some work to do each day and they were also going to arrange for a tutor to come round to the house for two hours, three times a week, but it was going to take a few days to sort out. In the meantime, Rachel went to speak to Shazia's family.

When she came round to see me afterwards she looked quite shaken up. Thankfully Shazia was upstairs in her bedroom when she arrived. I hadn't told Shazia that Rachel was going to see her family as I didn't want to add to her worry, and I knew I'd made the right decision when I saw Rachel's ashen face.

'How did it go?' I asked her.

'Her parents were fine,' she told me. 'Mum claimed they knew nothing about their sons trying to snatch Shazia from outside school. The brothers were a different kettle of fish, though.'

She explained how she had warned them not to approach Shazia and reminded them that Shazia didn't want to see or have contact with any of her family at the moment.

'What did they say?' I asked.

'Dev didn't say a lot, he just scowled at me and was generally trying to intimidate me. Adil, on the other hand, was very aggressive. He told me it was none of my business and to get out of the house. They became quite threatening and abusive so in the end I decided it was best to leave.'

Rachel had also been in touch with the police and told them about what had happened at school.

'Charge-wise they don't think there's anything worth pursuing, but DC Harris has agreed to go round and have a word with them and warn them that their intimidating behaviour and threats are unacceptable. She's also going reiterate the fact that they must not approach Shazia.'

'Hopefully they will get the message,' I sighed.

Everything that had happened at school had only added to my fear and it was clear that Shazia's family were not going to give up without a fight. My gut feeling now was that they would do whatever it took to get her back.

After everything that had happened, I was even more on my guard than I had been before and part of me was relieved that we would no longer have to make the twice-daily trips to and from school. But all I could think about was how long Shazia's brothers had been waiting outside her school. They must have been waiting for days, hoping to catch a glimpse of her. Had they been watching that morning when I'd dropped her off? Did they now know where I lived? What if they were waiting for their opportunity to strike?

At teatime I had a quick chat with Shazia and Louisa.

'Whenever we're in the house I want the chain to be on the door at all times just in case,' I told them.

'Why?' asked Shazia, looking panicked.

'After what happened at school I'm just being extra-cautious,' I explained.

I think Louisa thought I was being neurotic, but I could tell Shazia was still very shaken up by what had happened.

'They're not going to come here, are they?' she asked. 'They don't know where I am do they, Maggie?'

'I hope not, flower,' I told her. 'But I think from now on we all have to be on our guard. After today we can't assume anything.'

I'd been so distracted by what had been happening with Shazia that I was surprised when I got a call from Michael's social worker Helen later that week.

'How's it going, Maggie?' she asked.

'It's been a bit of a funny old week to say the least,' I sighed. 'But hopefully things have calmed down now. What can I do for you?'

Helen explained that she was ringing about Michael.

'As you know, he's been doing two overnights and four days a week at Kerry's house for the past month now,' she said. 'How do you think it's going?'

'Really well,' I told her. 'Michael seems happy and settled and he goes off with Kerry no problem. She seems to be coping fine with it.'

'That's great,' replied Helen. 'I've been round to visit her several times when she's had Michael there and I agree with you – things seems to be going really smoothly. I've talked to Kerry and she seems ready and happy to have Michel back full time. So I was thinking that perhaps next week could be Michael's last week with you.'

'Oh wow, that's so soon,' I gasped, failing to hide the surprise in my voice.

'Well, it's what we've been working towards since we upped the contact,' Helen reminded me.

'I know,' I said. 'And that's brilliant. It's just happened a bit sooner than I expected, that's all.'

Of course, I was delighted for Kerry and Michael and it would be great for him to be in the same place full time. It was the right thing to do and he was ready. He'd been going back and forth between mine and Kerry's for the past few weeks, sleeping in different cots in different houses. Now he needed to start making his own life in one place with his mother.

'I've agreed with Kerry that she can collect him Friday teatime and take him back permanently then.'

'Yes, that should be fine,' I told her.

It was yet another thing I needed to get my head around. As Michael was already spending a lot of time at Kerry's, I'd sorted through his stuff weeks ago and the majority of his things were already over there, so I didn't have much packing to do.

He'd been with me for over a year and although he was too young to understand what was happening, I wanted to mark his leaving with a little tea party.

That night I broke the news to Louisa.

'What, he's going so soon?' she sighed, her eyes filling with tears.

'That's exactly how I feel,' I told her. 'But we knew this day was coming.'

Shazia seemed just as upset as Louisa, even though she'd only known Michael for a few weeks.

'But how come he's leaving?' she asked. 'Why does he have to go?'

'He's going back to live with his mum Kerry,' I said. 'That was always the plan, so it's brilliant news for him.'

'But he's really cute and I like having him here, Maggie,' she sighed.

'I know, lovey,' I said. 'We're all going to miss him. I know it's hard, but it's happy news for Michael and we have to put our own feelings to one side and be pleased for him.'

I told the girls I was going to arrange a tea party for him on Friday afternoon.

'Can I help?' Shazia asked eagerly. 'I could make some samosas if you want?'

'Ooh, I love samosas,' said Louisa.

'That would be really nice,' I smiled.

At least helping me to plan the party would give Shazia something to keep her busy with until her tutor could start.

A couple of days later Helen called again.

'Is everything still set for next week?' I asked.

'Yes, I think so,' she said, sounding very vague.

She paused.

'Maggie, I'm not actually ringing about that. I need to talk to you about something else.'

She explained that the previous night, Social Services' out-of-hours duty team had taken an anonymous phone call claiming Kerry had been drunk while she was looking after Michael.

'Drunk?' I gasped.

'Maggie, have you got any concerns at all about Kerry and alcohol?' asked Helen. 'Have you seen anything that might suggest that she's drinking?'

'No,' I sighed, wracking my brains 'Nothing at all.'

I'd never smelt alcohol on her or suspected that she might be drunk. I'd never even seen her have a drink.

'When is this incident supposed to have happened?' I asked.

'The caller said Tuesday night,' Helen told me.

'But Kerry didn't have contact with Michael on Tuesday,' I told her. 'She couldn't have been drunk around him because he was here with me that night.'

It was a massive relief.

'As you know I still have a duty to check out any allegation so I'll have to talk to Kerry about it,' she said. 'The caller could have got the wrong day and Kerry might still be drinking. I know she's got Michael at home today so I'm going to go round there now and have a chat to her.'

I felt sick with worry at the thought of anything jeopardising Michael's return at the last minute. We'd all worked so hard to boost Kerry's confidence and help her believe that she could be a good enough mother to him. I knew her mental state was still fragile, and I was worried that this allegation, even if it were proven false, would lead to a crisis of confidence.

When Kerry came to drop Michael off that evening, I could tell she had been crying.

'Did Helen tell you what happened?' she asked, her thin shoulders shaking as she tried unsuccessfully to hold back her tears.

I nodded.

'I would never ever get drunk if I had Michael,' she sobbed. 'I don't even drink that often because of the medication I'm on.'

She explained that she had gone out to the local pub on Tuesday night.

'My cousin persuaded me to go as it was his birthday and Helen had just told me Michael was coming home so I was celebrating,' she told me, wiping away her tears with a trembling hand. 'For the first time in months I felt happy, Maggie, and to be honest I did get a bit merry.'

'And you're absolutely entitled to do that,' I reassured her.

'I promise I'd never do that if I had Michael with me,' she gulped. 'I swear, Maggie. I told Helen to check my flat. She wouldn't find any drink in there.'

I went and sat next to her on the sofa and gave her a hug.

'Do you think it means I'm not going to be allowed to have him back now?' she asked.

'Not at all,' I soothed. 'Helen has to check out an allegation like that, but it sounds like whoever made that call had got their facts completely wrong.'

'I bet I know who it was,' she sighed.

She explained that there were a couple of women who lived on her estate whose children had been taken into care.

'They've lost their kids to the social so I bet they're angry that I'm getting mine back,' she said. 'They've said a few nasty things to me over the past few weeks when they've seen me out with Michael.'

'It doesn't matter who made the allegations,' I told her. 'Helen will know by now that there's no truth in them.

'It's hard but try not to let it get to you,' I added. 'I've had lots of allegations made about me over the years and thankfully they've all turned out to be people just being bitter or bearing a grudge about something.'

'Really?' she said, looking surprised. 'Even you?'

'Even me,' I laughed.

I liked Kerry, I believed her, and I desperately hoped that she was telling the truth. That night, I tossed and turned, unable to sleep from worrying about it. I was relieved when Helen phoned the next morning.

'I've checked with the contact worker and the health visitor and nobody has ever smelled alcohol on Kerry or had any suspicions that she's been drinking,' she told me. 'I went round and saw her yesterday and she was absolutely gutted that someone had accused her of that.'

'I know,' I replied. 'She was very upset when she came here last night.'

'Her flat was clean and tidy and there wasn't any alcohol around that I could see,' continued Helen. 'So as far as I'm concerned, there isn't an issue. She went out and let her hair down, which she's perfectly entitled to do when she doesn't have Michael.'

I explained what Kerry had told me about the women on the estate.

'It sounds like it was probably just a case of sour grapes,' said Helen. 'But I did have to remind Kerry that once Michael is back with her, drinking is not a good idea.'

'She knows,' I assured her. 'She was devastated at the thought of something jeopardising her getting Michael back.'

I breathed a sigh of relief that things were back on track again and we could start planning for Michael to go home.

At the beginning of Michael's last week with us, I got an email to say a tutor was available to come and see Shazia. I could see Shazia was very nervous about it.

'What if they're really strict?' she asked me. 'I hope it's not a man. My parents wouldn't want me to have lessons on my own with a man.'

'Well unless you know any men called Glynis, I wouldn't worry,' I smiled. 'Don't worry. I'll always be in the house when she comes.'

Like most of the home tutors that I'd come across over the years, Glynis was a retired teacher. She was a sweet, grey-haired lady in her early sixties with a stick. But she was as sharp as a button and I could see she wasn't going to take any nonsense from Shazia.

Thankfully, she didn't ask me anything about why Shazia was in care or was being home-schooled.

'She seemed lovely,' I said to Shazia after she had gone.

'She's a bit old but she's nice,' she agreed.

It was going to be a busy week and my mind was buzzing with so many things – how Shazia was coping with the tutor after yet more change in her life and also adjusting to the fact that Michael was going to be leaving us in a matter of days.

When a child is leaving, everything becomes a countdown and ordinary, everyday events suddenly have a new, added poignancy. The morning before his final day I gave him a bath. As I watched him splashing and laughing and playing with his squeaky egg bath toys, a wave of sadness hit me.

His last bath at my house.

'Tomorrow's the big day,' I said when I dropped him off at Kerry's house. 'Are you excited?'

'I am,' she grinned. 'But I can hardly bring myself to believe it.'

She'd had everything ready for him months ago and the flat was looking immaculate.

'I've got him a special Paw Patrol balloon,' she whispered. 'But I've hidden it in the cupboard because I don't want him to see it until tomorrow.'

'Oh, he'll love that,' I smiled.

While I'd fostered Michael for over a year, I'd also known Kerry that long too, so it seemed only natural to invite her to the tea party.

'We'll see you when you bring him back tomorrow afternoon for the party,' I said.

'Yep,' she smiled. 'We're looking forward to it.'

With Michael at Kerry's for the last time overnight, it meant that in the morning, Shazia and I could throw ourselves into party planning so everything would be ready for the afternoon. Shazia was desperate to make her samosas as she had promised. They were very fiddly and I was impressed that she knew exactly what she was doing.

'Do you want me to deep-fry them for you?' I asked her, worried about her dealing with boiling oil.

'No, I can do it,' she said proudly.

'How do you know how to do all this?' I asked her.

'My mum taught me,' she said, sadly. 'We used to do all the cooking for my dad, uncles and brothers.'

She quickly looked away but not fast enough that I didn't notice the tears pricking her eyes.

Poor girl. I could see that she was still desperately confused about her feelings. On the one hand, she had so much anger towards her parents and what they had done to her. But on the other, they were still her family and she still felt that pull of loyalty and love.

'Do you miss your mum?' I asked her.

'No,' she said angrily. 'How could I love someone who was going to force me to get married and locked me up?'

But despite her words, her expression told me otherwise.

★

Shazia and I spent the rest of the day making sandwiches and baking cakes. I was glad of the opportunity to keep busy as it stopped me from focusing on what the party was for.

By 3 p.m. everything was ready for the guests to start arriving. Louisa had managed to leave work early and was bringing Charlie, and my friends Anne, Bob and Vicky were coming along.

Kerry arrived just after 3 p.m. with the guest of honour. Michael was dressed in a smart checked shirt and a gorgeous pair of navy cord dungaree shorts.

'Don't you look adorable,' I cooed, picking him up and using the opportunity to lavish him with kisses. He wriggled impatiently in my arms until I reluctantly put him down.

We all had a lovely afternoon.

'I bet you're counting down the hours until you can take him home forever,' I told Kerry.

'I still don't believe it's happening,' she sighed. 'It just feels like I'm taking him back for contact. It probably won't hit me for a few days.'

I was genuinely happy for her. Mental health is a complex issue and she had worked so hard to get herself strong enough that she could cope with having her son back.

'Someone's having a good time,' smiled Vicky as she gestured to Michael.

He was toddling around the room, a sausage roll in one hand, a chocolate cupcake in the other, babbling and smiling at everyone he passed. He had chocolate smeared around his mouth and crumbs from God knows what in his glossy curls.

'He's absolutely filthy,' I laughed.

It was then that I felt a familiar pang in my chest. The aching sensation of loss – sadly a feeling I knew only too well. I'd said goodbye to hundreds of children over the years, but it never ever got any easier. I'd learnt not to give myself a hard time about it, though. Once you'd formed an attachment with a child it was only natural to grieve for them once they had left. I'd watched Michael grow from a baby into a toddler. I'd done his night feeds, rocked him to sleep when he was poorly and seen him take his first steps. He'd gone from a frail little six-month-old to a curly-haired, chubby toddler who charmed everyone.

'You're going to miss that little lad, aren't you?' said Vicky, reaching for my hand and giving it a squeeze.

'I am,' I sighed, swallowing the lump in my throat.

Even though I'd got used to Michael spending a lot of time at Kerry's, I always looked forward to the nights he spent here. I would miss sitting in the rocking chair, reading him his favourite story *Goodnight Moon* and feeling his little body relaxing and getting all sleepy and heavy against me.

'It's time for him to be with his mummy,' I smiled, looking over at him. 'He deserves that.'

Just before 6 p.m. Kerry came over to me.

'Maggie, would you mind if I took Michael home?' she asked. 'He's getting tired and I want to give him a bath before I put him down to bed.'

'Of course,' I said. 'You don't need my permission. You're in charge now.'

There was no point in having a big goodbye as Michael was too young to understand that he was leaving us for good. He was used to leaving us to go to Kerry's for contact so in his little head he didn't know it was for the last time.

We all did though. I could see Louisa was doing her best to hold back the tears as she gave him a hug and a kiss.

'Miss you so much, little man,' she whispered, cuddling him close.

Suddenly Shazia ran over, picked Michael up and burst into tears.

'Oh Michael,' she sobbed. 'Please don't go.'

He was struggling in her arms and I could see he was desperate to be put down so I knew I had to intervene.

'Shazia, flower, it's OK,' I told her gently. 'Put him down now so Kerry can take him.'

'But it's not fair, I don't want him to go,' she cried, tears streaming down her face.

Louisa looked at me with a puzzled expression on her face, and I could tell she thought Shazia's reaction was a bit over the top.

'Give the baby to Kerry, lovey,' I repeated, more firmly this time.

Shazia handed him over and ran off upstairs in floods of tears.

'I'm sorry about that,' I told Kerry.

'It's OK,' she smiled. 'I know you're all going to miss him.'

Dealing with Shazia had distracted me from the inevitable. But now there was no putting it off. Kerry passed Michael to me and I gave him one last hug.

'Goodbye little fella,' I whispered, snuggling into his soft, warm neck for a final time. 'Go and be happy with your mummy.'

Then I lifted him into his buggy and helped strap him in to distract myself from crying.

'Thank you so much, Maggie,' said Kerry, giving me a hug. 'Thank you for everything. Without you I don't think I could have done this.'

Her voice was shaking with so much emotion she could hardly get the words out.

'Kerry, you don't have to thank me for anything,' I said, smiling at her. 'You did this. You're such a strong person and you should be so proud of yourself.

'Now get this boy out of here and get him to his bed in his lovely room,' I laughed.

'I would like us to stay in touch,' she told me. 'Would that be too weird for you? Will you come round and see us?'

'Of course we will,' I said. 'You and Michael get settled in for a few weeks and then give me a ring and we'll sort something out.'

'I will do,' she smiled. 'So it's not really goodbye then.'

'You're right,' I told her. 'It's more like see you soon.'

Louisa and I stood at the door and waved while she wheeled Michael down the path in his buggy. He was waving bye bye to us and blowing kisses with his chubby little fist just like Louisa had taught him.

'Oh he's dropped his cuddly monkey,' gasped Louisa as they walked off down the street. 'That's his favourite. Shall I go and pick it up?'

'Don't worry, I bet his mummy will notice,' I told her confidently.

As if on cue, Kerry looked down and realised the monkey was gone and ran back and picked it up off the pavement.

She was in charge now and I knew it was going to be fine.

'Come on, let's go in,' I told Louisa, suddenly shivering in spite of the warm summer night.

I was still nervous about standing out on the street and I knew I'd better go and check if Shazia was OK.

When I went upstairs to her room, she was lying on the bed bawling her eyes out.

'Oh lovey,' I said gently, going to sit down next to her. 'What's wrong?'

'I can't believe Michael's gone,' she cried, her face covered by the pillow. 'It's not fair, Maggie. Why can't he stay here with us?'

'Because he's gone to live with Kerry,' I told her. 'But we'll be OK. Things change. People move forward and life goes on.'

'But will I move on?' she said, looking at me with fearful brown eyes. 'What will I do, Maggie?'

For once I couldn't answer her.

THIRTEEN

Compassion Fatigue

The cot had been stripped, the windows had been cleaned and now I was busy taking down the curtains.

'What are you doing?' asked a curious voice from the doorway.

'Oh morning, lovey,' I smiled.

Shazia had just woken up and was standing there in her pyjamas and dressing gown.

'I'm giving Michael's room a bit of a spring clean,' I told her. 'I got up early so I've been hard at it since 7.30.'

'But why?' she asked sleepily.

'It's just something I do when a child moves on,' I told her. 'I like to keep myself busy to stop myself from feeling sad. I give everything a clean and a freshen up.'

Shazia sat down on the chair in the corner of the room and watched while I stood on a stepladder to take the curtains down.

'What's going to happen to me, Maggie?' she asked in a quiet voice. 'Will I have to move on too?'

'I honestly don't know yet, lovey,' I told her as I unhooked the curtain rings. 'In a few weeks Rachel will organise a meeting and we'll all sit down and talk about what's best for you.'

I had my back to Shazia, but instead of turning round, I fiddled with the curtain hooks and let her talk. I knew that sometimes children found it easier to share their feelings when they didn't have eye contact with you.

'But what about me?' she sighed. 'Will anyone ask what I want?'

'Of course they will,' I told her. 'Your views will be taken into consideration as well.'

I could see that Michael leaving had made Shazia worry about her own future. After everything that had happened in the past few days with her family, it was dawning on her that perhaps her new home needed to be somewhere far away from them. Somewhere far away from here.

'If I stay here with you and Louisa I'll never be safe, will I?' she sighed.

The hard thing was, at this point in time I couldn't give her any definite answers about her future, but she was right. She couldn't live from now until the age of eighteen having a tutor and hardly leaving the house. It was no life for a fourteen-year-old. She should be out and about with her friends, going places and enjoying her independence.

Now Michael had gone, it was just me and Shazia in the house during the day. Glynis the tutor came for two hours, three times a week. The safeguarding policy stated that whenever a child had a home tutor I always had to stay in the house during the session. The new routine felt very restrictive and we were pretty much confined to these four walls. We couldn't go out anywhere locally because of the risks of Shazia's family seeing us, but on the days Glynis was coming, we couldn't go further afield either as there wasn't enough time to drive somewhere out of the area and get back again before she arrived.

As I was quickly discovering, it was hard work trying to entertain a teenager 24/7. I didn't want to let her stay in bed all day or watch hours and hours of TV. With a little one you can spend ages making things, doing painting and Play-Doh and playing with toys. Although an older child is more independent, I found it much harder to think up things to keep Shazia busy. There's only so much cooking and baking and playing board games that you can do. It was such glorious weather so we felt even more trapped being inside. I'd force Shazia to go out into the garden and she'd sit on the swing just to get some fresh air. But I could see how bored and frustrated she was.

When we went out of town I'd always have to let Rachel know first. Sometimes on a day when Glynis wasn't coming we would drive to another city a couple of hours away just so we could have a walk around. We couldn't go to McDonald's or the cinema or shopping in our own town because all it would take would be for a cousin or someone in Shazia's family to see us and that would be it. Even when we did go out of the area I'd make sure Shazia didn't look distinctive. She wore mainly Western clothes now and was too frightened to put on a shalwar kameez when we went out in case it drew attention to herself.

Rachel called me one day to check how it was going with the new tutor.

'Shazia seems fine with her,' I told her. 'Obviously it's not the ideal long-term solution but she's happily doing the work that the school and Glynis have set.

'She's very aware of the fact that she's got GCSEs in a couple of years and she doesn't want to get behind with her school work.'

'That's great,' said Rachel. 'I'm pleased it's going well.'

'How are you finding her being at home?' she asked.

'I'm fine,' I sighed. 'I suppose I'm just finding it hard to entertain Shazia and on the days Glynis comes we often don't leave the house because we have to be back in the middle of the day.'

I was the kind of person who loved to get out and about. I was a great believer in fresh air and even when I had little babies to look after, I'd go out walking and take them to toddler groups from a young age. I wasn't one for sitting in the house all day so I'd started to feel quite confined.

That was one of the downsides of being a single carer. I didn't have anyone who could take over while I nipped out for a break.

Foster carers don't have the luxury that biological parents have where they can get grandparents, uncles or aunties to step in and have the children when they need a rest. That can happen when foster children are with you long term, but none of my family lived in the local area. As a single carer, I didn't have a partner to offload things on or to give me a break. I knew I was very lucky to have Louisa, but I was conscious of the fact she had her own life and it wasn't fair to rely on her to look after Shazia. However, I think she sensed my frustration and one afternoon she came home early from work.

'Why don't you nip out later?' she suggested. 'I can stay here with Shazia.'

'Are you sure?' I asked.

After the incident at Shazia's school I hadn't left her at all.

'Positive,' she replied. 'I'll put a DVD on and we can have some popcorn. I promise I won't open the door if anyone knocks.'

'OK,' I smiled. 'Thanks, lovey. I really appreciate that but I'll make sure I'm only gone for a couple of hours at the most.'

I texted Graham, who was delighted that I was unexpectedly available, and we arranged to meet at a country pub.

It was so nice to be out, but all the way through the meal I couldn't stop yawning.

'Am I keeping you awake?' he joked.

'I am sorry,' I told him. 'I don't know why I'm so tired. I haven't even been anywhere today.'

This was the first time I'd even left the house. But in a way, I was exhausted from not doing anything.

'It's tricky trying to amuse a teenager 24/7,' I told him. 'I hate not being able to get out and about.'

As a foster carer I'd learnt that it was important to have time away from the children I was looking after. Even a trip to Asda at 9 p.m. at night, when everyone was in bed and Louisa was looking after them, felt like a holiday. Even though I was just doing the shopping, at least I was on my own, and mentally and emotionally, it was time away from everyone at home. But I hadn't even dared to do that lately after everything that had happened to Shazia.

A couple of days later there was a coffee morning at my fostering agency and I was determined to go. The offices were five minutes from my house and nowhere near where Shazia's parents lived, so Rachel had deemed it OK.

'A coffee morning?' sighed Shazia. 'I don't want to go to that. It's so boring. It will just be babies.'

'I thought you liked babies?' I said.

She was determined to make a point so when we got to my agency, she sat in reception rather than come into the room where the coffee morning was being held.

'Where's Shazia?' asked Becky when she saw me.

'Having a sulk out there,' I said.

I knew she would be safe as it was a secure area that you needed a pass to get into and I'd asked the receptionist to keep an eye on her.

I couldn't be too hard on her. I knew Shazia was finding it difficult being in the house so much too, and I knew that she missed Zeena and going to school. I didn't stay long but just as I was about to leave, Becky pulled me to one side.

'Are you OK, Maggie?' she asked, a worried look on her face. 'You don't seem your normal chirpy self.'

'Yes, I'm fine,' I told her, surprised. 'I'm just a bit tired, that's all. I'm not sure why as I've only got Shazia in placement at the moment.'

'Well, you take care and let me know if it gets too much,' she told me.

'I'll be fine,' I said, dismissing her concern.

A couple of days later Becky called me.

'Maggie, we've got a referral for two little girls – an eight- and nine-year-old,' she told me. 'I thought it would be right up your street. Do you fancy it?'

Normally I would have bitten her arm off but I felt utterly exhausted.

'Becky, I don't know what's wrong with me,' I told her.

'But I don't think I can take any more children on at the moment. I can't do it.'

I actually felt quite tearful which surprised me.

'Maggie, are you going to be in later?' she asked. 'I'd like to pop in for a coffee.'

'I'm always around at the moment,' I told her sadly. 'I can't go anywhere.'

A couple of hours later Becky was standing on my doorstep.

'I've never heard you like that before,' she said, her voice etched with concern. 'I'm worried about you, Maggie. It's not like you to turn down a placement.'

'I can't bring two children into this environment when we haven't even got the freedom to walk to the local park,' I told her. 'It wouldn't be fair.'

'If I'm honest, I'm climbing the walls here, Becky,' I added, my eyes filling with tears. 'But I can't complain because I know Shazia is finding it hard too.'

'Maggie, you should have told me this was how you're feeling,' she scolded, patting my hand. 'I would have been able to do something about it.'

'I don't understand why I'm so exhausted when I haven't been doing anything,' I told her, wiping a tear from my eye. 'And I'm not normally a crier, am I?'

'No, you're not,' she laughed. 'In all seriousness it sounds like you've got a bit of compassion fatigue.'

Compassion fatigue is the stress you can feel caring for someone who has experienced trauma. It can affect you physically or emotionally, or both.

'But Michael's gone, so all I've got is Shazia,' I replied. 'As you know I've had way more placements than that.'

'Yes, but in a weird way, the fewer children you have, the more you might feel it because you've got the time to,' she told me. 'Maggie, you're only human. You and I both know from experience it's not possible to give yourself over to a child 24/7.

'I think being stuck indoors with Shazia day in and day out is too much. It's too intense. You need a break,' she said. 'How about I have a chat to Vicky and see if she can take her for one day a week?'

'No way,' I said. 'That's not necessary. Vicky's got enough on her plate. She's got three kids with her at the moment. It's not like I'm rushed off my feet.'

'Maggie, there's nothing wrong in accepting help,' Becky told me firmly. 'I've known you long enough to know when there's something wrong. You're not yourself.'

Compassion fatigue is something rarely talked about among foster carers and is only now just starting to be recognised by professionals. Carers often don't realise they've got it, but it leaves them feeling exhausted and burnt out. For me it was about having somebody around who was constantly emotionally reliant and dependent upon me. Yes, babies and small children were hard work and tiring, but they had naps and went to nursery or school, which provided much-needed breaks. People sometimes put foster carers on a pedestal, but we're only human and looking after children who have been through traumatic experiences can be intense. Sometimes we all need a break.

In Shazia's case, the trauma I was facing was living with the daily fear of 'What if'. I felt so responsible for her safety that even in my own home I was on high alert. No matter what room of the house we were in, I was constantly thinking about what my contingency plan was. What if someone threw a brick through the window of the front bedroom? What if somebody came to the door and started smashing their way in? What if she looked out of the window and at that particular moment one of her family was driving past and saw her?

I felt like my job had stopped being a foster carer and now I was a prison officer or bodyguard. Every minute of every day I was checking where Shazia was and what she was doing. I was even conscious of the fact that I was happier when she was upstairs in the house and I was downstairs than if it was the other way around. That way I knew her brothers would get to me first and not her if they were to break in.

When we went out, I was always weighing up the situation too. Even when we went to a city two hours away, I would look for the emergency exits in shops and restaurants so I knew we could make a quick getaway if needed.

'Perhaps you're right,' I told Becky reluctantly. 'Maybe I'm so shattered because I'm continually on edge.'

So I relented and Vicky agreed to have Shazia one day a week on a day when she didn't have the tutor.

Shazia wasn't very happy about it when I told her.

'But why do I have to go?' she groaned. 'It'll be so boring.'

'There are lots of things I need to do locally that I'm not able to do when I'm with you,' I told her. 'I need to get shopping, I need to do some banking and go and sort things. I can do all that on one particular day each week and I know you're going to be safe at Vicky's.'

She would just have to accept it.

The first time she went to Vicky's, I still felt guilty leaving her.

'Maggie, she will be absolutely fine,' Vicky reassured me. 'You go and enjoy the break.'

I must admit I didn't have anything planned that day. It was warm and sunny and I walked into town. I felt so free being able to go where I wanted and not be worried about who I was going to see. I got a coffee from a café and sat on a bench in the park, watching people go by. It felt good to feel the sun on my face and breathe in the fresh air. If my own four walls were driving me demented, God knows what they were doing to Shazia.

When I went to pick up Shazia, I was relieved when Vicky assured me that everything had been fine.

'We didn't do much, but I think it's been good for her to have a change of scene,' she told me.

'There is one thing I wanted to mention,' she said discreetly.

She said that Shazia had been going to the toilet continually and had been ages each time.

'When I asked her what was wrong she said it was tummy ache. I just thought I'd mention it.'

'Thanks Vicky,' I said. 'She always takes ages in the toilet but I'll have a chat with her when I get home. It might be the time of the month.'

That evening I also noticed she was up and down to the loo.

'Are you OK, flower?' I asked her. 'You're going to the toilet an awful lot. Vicky mentioned you were the same at her house too.'

'Maggie, my tummy aches and it really stings when I try and go for a wee,' she said.

'Oh, you poor thing,' I soothed. 'It sounds like you might have another urine infection. I'll phone the doctors in the morning and try and get you an appointment.'

'Can it be a lady doctor?' she asked.

'Yes, of course,' I nodded.

I phoned first thing and managed to get an appointment.

The doctor agreed that it sounded like a bladder infection when Shazia told her her symptoms.

'I'll need you to go and do a urine sample for me so I can confirm it,' she said, handing her a pot.

I stayed with the doctor while Shazia went off to the loo.

Five minutes passed. Then ten minutes.

'Do you think she's OK?' the GP asked. 'She's been a very long time.'

'This is normal for her,' I told her. 'She spends ages in the loo. Sometimes she can be half an hour or more.'

Shazia finally came back twenty minutes later.

'Did you struggle to get a sample?' the GP asked her.

'No,' she said. 'It was fine.'

The GP looked concerned.

'I'll give you some antibiotics, but as it's your second infection in as many months, I'd like to refer you to a consultant,' she said. 'We need to try and find out if there's a reason that you keep getting them and also why it takes you so long to go to the toilet.'

'Do I have to?' she asked, looking worried. 'I've always been like that.'

'I think the doctor's right,' I reassured her. 'It's just worth a check to make sure that everything's OK. It's nothing to worry about and I'll come with you to the appointment.'

Ever since Shazia had come to live with me I'd been struck by the length of time that she spent in the bathroom, and I was relieved that the GP shared my concerns. But little did I know what a simple appointment was about to uncover.

FOURTEEN

Tradition or Torture

As I pulled into the hospital car park, I could see Shazia was getting more and more anxious.

'What will she do again?' she asked, nervously fiddling with the buttons on her blouse. 'And it will be a woman won't it?'

Amazingly, we'd got an appointment with a paediatric urologist just two weeks after our appointment with the GP, even though I'd expected it to take months.

'She'll probably check your tummy and ask you a few questions,' I reassured her. 'Don't worry, I'll be there with you and she won't do anything without your permission. She just needs to check if there's any reason why you keep getting these infections.'

I could see that Shazia was nervous about it. I was nervous about the appointment too but for a very different reason. There was only one main hospital in the local area and I hoped that we weren't going to bump into any of Shazia's family while we were there.

Luckily we didn't have to wait long and I relaxed a little bit once we were in the safety of the consultant's room.

She was a softly spoken woman in her fifties who had a gentle, calm manner and I could see that she immediately put Shazia at ease.

'You must be Shazia,' she smiled. 'I'm Melanie Turner.'

'I'm Maggie Hartley, Shazia's foster carer,' I said, introducing myself.

She scanned through the notes she'd got from the GP.

'First of all, I'd like to do an ultrasound of your kidneys and bladder and then I'll have a feel of your stomach,' she explained.

'Will it hurt?' asked Shazia, alarmed.

'No, it shouldn't do,' the consultant smiled. 'The gel I put on your stomach to run the ultrasound over might be a little bit cold but that should be the worst of it.'

Poor Shazia still looked terrified as she lay down on the bed to be scanned.

The consultant lifted up her top and pulled down her leggings slightly.

'The good news is that it all looks clear and I can't see anything at all to be concerned about,' she said. 'I'd like to examine you now if that's OK, Shazia. I need to have a feel of your stomach and then have a look internally.'

'I'll pull this curtain around you while you take your knickers and leggings off,' she explained. 'Then I want you to lie on the couch for me. There's a sheet there that you can put over your bottom half for privacy.'

Shazia looked terrified.

'Don't worry,' I told her, desperately trying to reassure her. 'It's not going to hurt and I'll be right here on the other side of the curtain.'

The examination took about ten minutes and I could hear the consultant gently talking her through everything that she was doing although Shazia never said a word.

'Good girl,' she said finally. 'You can get dressed now.'

The consultant came out from behind the curtain and my stomach sank. I took one look at the grim expression on her face and I knew instantly that something was terribly wrong.

But there was no time to ask any questions as a few minutes later Shazia emerged, fully dressed and looking relieved that the examination was over and done with.

'Well done,' I smiled. 'Hopefully that wasn't as bad as you thought.'

'Shazia, do you want to wait outside in reception while I have a quick word with your foster carer?' the consultant told her.

'OK,' she said eagerly, obviously delighted to be getting out of there.

As soon as the door closed, I turned to the consultant.

'What is it?' I asked. 'What did you find?'

'I think what's happening is her scar tissue is getting infected,' she told me. 'It's been very crudely sewn so that could be what's causing the recurrent problems. Unfortunately these sorts of procedures can lead to regular urine infections amongst other things.'

I looked at her blankly. I didn't have a clue what she was talking about.

'Sorry?' I asked, puzzled. 'Scar tissue? What procedure are you talking about?'

The consultant's face fell.

'Oh my goodness, I'm so sorry,' she gasped. 'I assumed that you knew.'

'Knew what?' I asked, getting more and more alarmed by the minute. 'Will you please explain to me what you're talking about?'

'So you're not aware that Shazia has been subjected to a procedure called FGM?'

'FGM?' I repeated, even more confused now.

'Female Genital Mutilation,' she replied.

I'd heard the term before but I couldn't pretend that I knew exactly what it was.

'I think I've read something about that in a newspaper once,' I said vaguely.

'It's a procedure that involves part or total removal of the outer female genitals,' she explained. 'Some people call it female circumcision.'

My head started to spin as I struggled to take in the full horror of what she was telling me.

'Female circumcision?' I gasped. 'Isn't that something that's done in Africa?'

At that point in time, several years ago, FGM wasn't as widely known or talked about as it is now. It certainly wasn't something that I had come across in my day-to-day life. Naively, perhaps, I couldn't believe that it was something girls like Shazia, who had been born and brought up in the UK, were subjected to.

'Sadly it's carried out in many countries around the world,' the consultant told me. 'On girls from many different cultures. Unfortunately it looks like Shazia has been subjected to the most severe kind.'

I was so shocked, I honestly didn't know what to say. I listened in absolute horror as she described how Shazia's vaginal opening had been narrowed.

'It's a very crude technique where they create a sort of seal using the girl's labia,' she told me. 'That explains why she takes so long in the toilet and has been getting so many kidney infections. She's very lucky that she hasn't experienced any other more serious complications so far.'

'That poor, poor girl,' I sighed, shaking my head.

I couldn't believe what I was hearing and what Shazia had been subjected to. I had so many questions but I didn't know where to start.

'When would this have been done to her?' I asked.

'Judging by the scar tissue I would guess that Shazia had this done quite a few years ago as a young child,' she said. 'I believe the most common time is around three to five years old.'

It was utterly barbaric.

'Has she mentioned anything to you?' she asked.

I shook my head.

'There's a possibility that she doesn't even know,' she told me. 'Especially if it was something that was done when she was three or four. She might not remember.'

'I honestly don't think she does,' I told her. 'She seems to think it's normal to spend a long time going to the loo.

'There's no mention of it in any of the paperwork or reports from Social Services. I don't think any of us were aware of this. It's come completely out of the blue.'

'Do you want to bring Shazia back in so I can talk to her about it?' the consultant suggested. 'I'm happy to explain it to her and try to answer her questions.'

My head was spinning as I tried to work out what was the best thing to do.

'To be honest, this has totally floored me,' I sighed. 'I've never ever come across a situation like this before or a child who has had this procedure done to them. I think I need to talk to Shazia's social worker first before we speak to her and work out with her how best to handle it.'

'That's understandable,' said the consultant, smiling sympathetically. 'I know this must be a huge shock for you. These kinds of cases are always shocking for me to see and I've only dealt with three over a twenty-year career.

'There's a consultant I know at another hospital who specialises in reconstructive surgery for girls who have gone through this,' she told me. 'He knows a lot more about FGM than I do, so I can put you in touch with him if you like?'

'Thanks, that would be really helpful,' I replied. 'The more information we have, the better.'

I was hoping that Rachel knew more about FGM than I did or had dealt with other cases in the past because I totally felt out of my depth here.

'As you're probably aware, FGM is against the law so I'm going to have to report this to the police,' she said. 'Obviously it might be less of an urgent situation because Shazia has already been removed from her birth family's care, but it needs investigating nevertheless.'

'Yes, of course,' I told her. 'I completely understand. I'll give you Shazia's social worker's details as she's the best person for them to contact initially. Obviously we would want to tell her first before she was questioned by the police.'

I wrote down Rachel's email address and phone number.

'What are you going to tell Shazia for now?' the consultant asked me.

'I don't want to lie to her,' I said. 'But I don't think I can tell her anything right now. I really do feel like I need to talk to her social worker first as this is such new territory for me.'

As I walked down the corridor towards the waiting room, I took a few deep breaths and tried to compose myself. I felt like crying at the barbarity of what Shazia had been put through. I was absolutely horrified and appalled that her own family had allowed this to happen to her.

In my eyes, it was mutilation. Plain and simple.

I felt so protective of this young girl who had been through so much. I wanted to run into the waiting room and scoop her up into my arms, but I knew that at this point in time I had to keep the information to myself. I felt guilty not telling Shazia straight away, as after all, this was her body, but I was in such a strange, unknown situation that I wanted to take professional advice and make sure that we handled it in the best possible way. Shazia was already so vulnerable after everything that had happened to her at the hands of her family. I knew that this might tip her over the edge.

I swallowed the lump in my throat as I walked into the waiting room and saw Shazia flicking through a magazine.

'You've been ages,' she sighed. 'I was dead bored.'

'I was just talking to the consultant about a few things,' I told her, trying to keep my voice as chirpy as possible. 'She wants you to make sure you drink lots of water to keep your kidneys flushed out.'

'I told you there was nothing wrong with me,' she smiled happily.

I honestly didn't know what to say in reply.

'Come on then, we'd better get back,' I told her briskly.

In the car, I put the radio on in the hope that we could avoid conversation. My mind was reeling, still trying to absorb the bombshell that the consultant had dropped.

'Is Glynis coming today?' asked Shazia on the drive home.

'Oh yes, you're right,' I replied, startled out of my thoughts.

She was due half an hour after we got back and in a way, it was perfect timing. If Shazia was with Glynis, it would give me chance to speak to Rachel privately about what had happened at the hospital.

As soon as I walked through the front door I sent her a text.

Hi Rachel, I need to speak to you urgently re Shazia. Please could you pop round in the next couple of hours?

She replied quickly saying she was in a meeting but could come and see me in an hour.

Hope all is OK, she replied.

Not really, I thought to myself.

I just had time to make Shazia some lunch before Glynis arrived. Ten minutes later, the doorbell rang again.

It was too early to be Rachel so I nervously opened the door with the chain still on.

'It's only me,' she smiled. 'My meeting finished early so I thought I'd come straight round.'

The minute she saw my face she knew there was something dreadfully wrong.

'Maggie, what is it?' she asked. 'What's happened?'

I felt so horrified, so choked up about everything that I'd been told at the hospital this morning that I burst into tears.

'Oh Maggie,' she said, putting her arm around me. 'You're making me really worried now. What is it?'

I struggled to find the words to tell her what the consultant had discovered and the horror that Shazia had been through.

'Oh my God,' she gasped, clasping her hand over her mouth. 'That poor girl.'

Unlike me, Rachel knew instantly what FGM was. Now all social workers have training in FGM and how to deal with it, but at that point in time it wasn't something that was widely known about.

'I've just read a book about this,' she told me. 'It was a Somalian model who'd had this procedure done to her. It's just horrendous.'

'That's exactly how I feel,' I sighed. 'I can't get my head around it. Why would a parent agree for that to be done to their child?'

'There are all sorts of cultural reasons,' Rachel sighed. 'Do you think Shazia knows that this has been done to her?'

I shook my head. 'I honestly don't. The consultant said it's sometimes carried out when girls are three or four so she might not even remember. What on earth do we do now, Rachel?' I asked. 'How do we tell her this? It's been so hard not saying anything to her and that's only since we've left the hospital. How do we break this to her?'

For the first time in my fostering career, I was in completely unknown territory.

'Thankfully, I've never had to deal with this situation before either,' she sighed. 'I need to go back to the office and get some advice from my manager about how best to proceed.'

'OK,' I told her. 'We're going to have to tell her sooner rather than later. I can't keep important information like this from her. It's her body and she has a right to know. Plus the consultant has a professional duty to report it to the police so they might want to talk to her.'

'I agree,' Rachel nodded. 'She needs to be told as soon as possible. However, we want to make sure we do it in the most sensitive and informative way that we can.'

It was hard pretending to Shazia that nothing was wrong and acting normally. Every time I looked at her I wanted to cry. From what little I knew so far, I understood that she was going to live with the ramifications of this for the rest of her life.

Rachel called back later that afternoon.

'I've spoken to my manager,' she said. 'We both feel the best course of action is if you and I go and see the FGM specialist that the consultant mentioned. I think the more information we have, the better, and that way we can be fully equipped to answer Shazia's questions.'

'I agree,' I said. 'We need to get our own heads around it before we tell her.'

Rachel said she had already called the consultant and explained the situation and had arranged for us to go and see him on Monday.

'It's when Shazia will be at Vicky's, I think, so I'd really appreciate it if you could come too. I think we both need to work out a way to tell Shazia together and the consultant will be able to give us all the facts rather than us relying on the internet for all the answers.'

'I agree,' I nodded.

Throughout the weekend I felt guilty for hiding something from Shazia, but I knew I had no other option and was doing it for all the right reasons.

On Monday Rachel and I drove up to the hospital to see the consultant.

Paul Moss was a friendly-looking man with a beard. All I could think about was how horrific it must be to deal with what he saw on a daily basis.

'Thank you for agreeing to see us,' Rachel told him as we sat down.

'No problem,' he said. 'When Melanie explained what had happened I was happy to have a chat with you, and hopefully it will help,' he told us. 'I can certainly give you the facts, but sadly they don't make easy listening.'

Over the next half an hour, he explained very matter-of-factly how FGM was the removal of all or part of the external female genitals for non-medical reasons.

'There are no health benefits to it whatsoever,' he said. 'It's mainly done for cultural reasons. It's often something women in that family have had done to them for generations.'

'It's not tradition,' I sighed. 'It's torture.'

'I completely agree with you,' he said. 'In my mind it equates to child abuse.'

'But why would any parent allow this to be done to their daughter?' asked Rachel.

'All sorts of reasons,' replied Paul. 'Parents from these communities often feel a great deal of pressure to agree to it. It could be something that's been done for generations in their family and has become tradition. Often they feel it's the best thing they can do for their daughter's marriageable status. It's seen as a positive thing as it makes her more marriageable. It could be that in their community whoever they marry will pay a higher dowry for a girl who has had this done.'

He also described how it meant women who had had FGM wouldn't experience sexual pleasure and this would keep them 'chaste'.

'In some areas of the world, girls who don't have FGM are seen as unclean and promiscuous and because of that they're seen as social outcasts,' he said.

He also ran through the possible complications that it could cause.

'The girl you're fostering is lucky to have even survived the operation,' he told us. 'FGM is often carried out abroad by unqualified villagers in unsanitary conditions without any pain relief. Many girls die during the procedure and it can often cause death and disability.'

It was so hard to comprehend and I felt my eyes filling up with tears.

'Girls can still have periods, but there are all sorts of medical complications such as pain and constant infections,' he continued. 'It makes sex and childbirth extremely difficult and dangerous.'

'But is there anything that can be done to reverse it?' I asked.

'It's best to try and get Shazia to deal with what's happened to her emotionally first,' he said. 'I wouldn't recommend surgery until she's been through puberty and come to terms with things a little bit more. Later down the line, she might want to consider reconstructive surgery to open up the scar tissue. It can't replace anything that's been removed, but it can help make things more comfortable.

'I'm happy to talk to her with you if you think that would help?' he offered.

'That's very kind of you,' said Rachel. 'But I think it's something that has to come from Maggie and me initially.'

We both walked out of there feeling that we had a lot more information but were equally shell-shocked at the brutality of it all.

'I'll get the ball rolling and start to organise some counselling ASAP to enable her to try and properly understand it and process it,' said Rachel grimly.

But we both knew what we needed to do now. The time had come to tell Shazia what had happened to her, and neither of us had any idea how she was going to react.

FIFTEEN

Explanations

Rachel and I sat in silence in the hospital café, staring into our cups of coffee.

'How on earth do we tell her?' I sighed.

How did we break the news to her that her parents had allowed this barbaric thing to be done to her and now she had to live with the consequences of their decision for the rest of her life?

'I honestly don't know,' replied Rachel, stirring a sugar lump into her cup. 'All we can do is be honest with Shazia and present her with the facts and try to answer any questions that she might have.

'Maybe when we talk to her about it we'll find out that she knows that she's had it done?' she added hopefully.

I shook my head.

'I wish that was the case, but I'm convinced that she doesn't know,' I said. 'I think this is going to be a huge shock for her, especially after everything else that she's had to cope with lately.'

Rachel was still struggling to find a counsellor who had experience with FGM and could work with Shazia to help her process her feelings.

'It might take a while,' she told me. 'But I think for now, we need to get on with telling Shazia.'

'She needs to know,' I agreed. 'The sooner the better, really.'

Rachel agreed to come round later that afternoon when Shazia was back from Vicky's house. I knew it needed to happen, but that didn't stop me from dreading it. FGM was something that I was struggling to comprehend as a grown woman, never mind a fourteen-year-old girl who would have to live with its effects for the rest of her life.

I casually mentioned to Shazia that Rachel was going to pop round and ten minutes later she was on the doorstep. Rachel looked as apprehensive as I felt, and we gave each other a weak smile as she walked into the hallway.

'Shall we go and sit in the front room?' she suggested.

'Oh, it must be something dead serious if you want us to go in there and not the kitchen,' laughed Shazia.

Rachel and I looked at each other and it was clear that Shazia could sense that something important was happening. She went very quiet and stared at us both, wide-eyed.

She flopped down on the sofa and I sat next to her. I honestly didn't know how she was going to react to what we had to tell her. Would there be anger or tears perhaps? Or just sadness and confusion? Shazia had been brought up in a culture where your body was private and wasn't talked about, so I knew this whole conversation was going to be very uncomfortable for her. I remembered reading in the Social Services' reports when she'd arrived with me that her parents had asked for her to be taken out of the classroom during sex education.

As Shazia's social worker, we'd already agreed that Rachel would be the one to take the lead and I would be there for backup and support.

My heart was in my mouth as Rachel started to talk.

'Shazia, there's something really important that Maggie and I need to speak to you about,' she began. 'Remember when you went to see the consultant at the hospital last week with Maggie?'

Shazia nodded.

'Well, when the doctor was examining you, she found something,' she continued.

'Was it cancer?' interrupted Shazia, looking horrified. 'Have I got cancer? My auntie had that. Am I going to die?'

'No, sweetie, you haven't got cancer,' I reassured her. 'Listen to what Rachel's telling you.'

Rachel cleared her throat and continued.

'She could tell from examining you that when you were little, you'd had a procedure carried out on you called FGM,' she told her. 'It stands for Female Genital Mutilation.'

Shazia looked at her blankly.

'What procedure?' she asked. 'What does that mean? What's a genital?'

Rachel explained as simply and as matter of factly as she could exactly what FGM was and what had been done to her body. The consultant had given us some leaflets that also included some diagrams that we thought might help Shazia understand as her knowledge of her body at this age was going to be limited.

Her eyes widened with shock and confusion as she looked at them and it slowly started to sink in.

'I've had this?' she asked, her face contorted with horror.

'Do you remember anything like this ever happening to you when you were little?' I asked her gently. 'Do you remember having some sort of operation, maybe when you went to Pakistan?'

Shazia shook her head.

'No,' she said. 'We went to Pakistan every summer but I don't remember anything like that. Would it have hurt?'

'It probably would have done,' said Rachel. 'It depends how and where it was done.'

I could see that Shazia was struggling to take it all in.

'Are you sure it's true?' she asked. 'My bits have always been like this. I didn't think I was different to anyone else. Maybe that lady got it wrong?'

'The consultant is very sure,' nodded Rachel. 'She could clearly see that a large section of your vagina had been sewn up and that explains why you keep getting urine infections.'

I could see that Shazia was embarrassed.

'It's nothing to be ashamed of, lovey,' I assured her. 'Now we know what's happened to you we can talk about it and work out what's best.'

'I don't want to talk about it,' she yelled. 'I don't care what's been done to me. It doesn't matter.'

'Shazia, we need to talk about it,' I pleaded. 'You need to realise that this procedure is going to affect you for the rest of your life.'

'But how?' she asked, her brow furrowed with worry.

The truth was harsh but she needed to know it.

'I know that you're not sexually active now but it can cause problems when you're older and want to have sex,' I told her. 'It might also affect you being able to give birth safely.'

'What, you mean I can't have babies?' she asked, looking distraught.

'Hopefully you can,' Rachel told her. 'There are lots of things that can be done to try and help you. There's a consultant who specialises in operating on girls who like you who've had FGM,' she told her. 'Maggie and I went to see him and he's happy to talk to you and answer any questions that you might have.'

'No way,' said Shazia. 'I told you, I don't want to talk about it and I'm definitely not talking to some strange bloke about what's happened to my bits. It's disgusting.'

With that, she threw the leaflets to the floor, stood up and stormed out of the room. We heard her stomp up the stairs and her bedroom door slammed shut above us.

'I feel so sorry for her,' sighed Rachel, picking up the information from the floor. 'It's such a huge thing for her to cope with on top of everything else.'

'At least she knows now,' I told her.

My heart was breaking for Shazia. It was such a hard thing to try and get her head around.

During the conversation, one thing had stood out for me though.

'She never asked why,' I said to Rachel. 'She didn't want to know why her parents would have allowed her to have it done.'

'I'm sure that will come in time,' she said. 'The next few days are going to be a bit of a rollercoaster ride for you Maggie, I'm afraid.'

I feared that she was right.

When Rachel had gone, I went upstairs to check on Shazia.

I gently tapped on her bedroom door.

'Go away,' she shouted. 'I don't want to talk to you.'

'Shazia, I just want to check that you're OK and have a chat to you.'

'I'm sick of talking,' she hissed. 'Leave me alone.'

I knew I had to respect her wishes. She needed time and space to try and take it all in and then hopefully she would open up to me. I pushed the information that Rachel had brought under her bedroom door in the hope that she would read it if she wanted to.

An hour later, Shazia eventually came downstairs. She looked exhausted and I could tell from her puffy red eyes that she'd been crying.

'Are you alright, flower?' I asked her.

She nodded.

'I know this is embarrassing for you but if you've got any questions, you know you can ask me anything,' I told her.

'I don't want to talk about it,' she said, looking at the floor.

She didn't eat much dinner that evening, and she hardly said a word. I chatted away about nonsense to try and fill the silence, but I didn't mention anything about FGM. I didn't want to push her or keep asking her if she was OK as the day had been traumatising enough for her already.

Later on we watched TV. Halfway through an episode of *EastEnders*, Shazia turned to me.

'Why would my mum and dad make me have that thing done, Maggie?' she asked, her eyes shiny with tears. 'Why would they let someone do that to me when I was so little?'

I picked up the remote control and turned off the TV so we could talk properly.

'It's complicated,' I told Shazia. 'And that's a hard question for me to answer without being able to chat to your parents about it. But from what I've learnt about FGM, it could be that it's the tradition in the community where your parents are from that girls have this done. Your parents probably thought they were doing their best for you and they might not have understood the consequences.

'Girls who have had FGM are sometimes considered more marriageable and pure than those who haven't, so maybe they believed they were doing a good thing.'

I knew I couldn't project my own feelings and emotions onto her, no matter how hard it was to stay neutral. I wanted to tell her that in my eyes and the eyes of the law, FGM was child abuse. That, tradition or not, it was barbaric and had no place in our or any other society. I wanted to tell her that young girls were dying, being mutilated and left disabled all in the name of this tradition designed to stop them from having sex before marriage and to keep them faithful during marriage. But I had to keep my mouth firmly shut, give Shazia the facts and not express my own personal opinion. It wasn't fair to openly criticise Shazia's culture or her parents in front of her. I didn't understand why anyone would allow their young daughter to be butchered like that, but I knew that Shazia needed to come to her own conclusions.

Over the next few days, I didn't mention FGM unless Shazia did. She was very quiet and even Glynis the tutor noticed it.

'She doesn't seem her usual self,' she told me discreetly on the way out one afternoon. 'Is she feeling OK?'

'She had some bad news last week,' I explained. 'So she's dealing with a lot at the moment.'

One morning, Shazia was tucking into her porridge and I was making toast when she suddenly started to talk.

'Maggie, I think I remember going to Pakistan one time and being really poorly,' she said. 'I had to stay in bed for most of the holiday and I felt really hot and sick. Would that be it?' she asked. 'Do you think when they did that thing to me it would have made me ill?'

'It could have done, sweetie,' I told her.

By the end of the week, Rachel had found a counsellor and got funding confirmed for six sessions.

'Aisha's originally from Somalia and she mainly works with Somali girls in the UK who have had this done,' she told me. 'She's lovely and I think Shazia will really like her.'

Rachel had arranged for her to have two one-hour sessions a week.

'I thought Shazia would be more comfortable and at ease having the sessions at your house,' she told me.

'That's fine,' I said.

I wasn't sure how Shazia was going to take the idea of counselling.

'Why are you all so desperate for me to talk about it?' she moaned. 'I'm tired of talking.'

'Even if you don't talk to this lady, then at least listen to what she has to say,' I told her. 'She's dealt with lots of girls who've experienced FGM so she'll know a lot more than Rachel or I do.'

'Do I have to?' Shazia sighed.

'Try it,' I pleaded. 'Just for me.'

Aisha came round for the first session the next day. I'd been expecting an older woman, but she was in her thirties and fashionably dressed, wearing a flamboyant silk scarf tied around her head and red lipstick. I could see Shazia was impressed by her.

'How did it go?' I asked Aisha afterwards.

I knew that because of confidentiality she couldn't tell me what Shazia had said, but I was keen to know how she'd coped with the session.

'I think it helped her to know that she's not alone,' she told me. 'That she's not a freak. She was gobsmacked when I explained that around 95 per cent of Somalian girls between 4 and 11 have had FGM.

'There were a few tears at some points but that's no surprise,' she added. 'It's a lot for her to cope with.'

Shazia seemed to have really warmed to Aisha.

'Did you find that useful?' I asked her.

'She was cool,' was all she was willing to tell me. 'I liked her.'

I think speaking to Aisha had helped her to understand the long-term implications of FGM. After one of the sessions she came to me in a panic.

'Maggie, I need to have that operation done to reverse it,' she told me, looking terrified. 'I don't want anyone to hurt me.'

'There's no rush to do anything like that, lovey,' I soothed. 'We can't do anything straightaway and you're still young. We can talk to the consultant and get a referral.'

'Yes,' she said. 'That's what I want.'

'Aisha said it's normal that I don't remember,' she told me. 'She said it might have been so traumatic that I've blocked it out or they might have knocked me out. She said the memories might come back later on but I'm not sure I want them to.'

I thought it was probably better that she didn't ever remember.

What had happened to Shazia was so personal and so shocking that I hadn't even shared it with Louisa. One night, however, she came to me in tears.

'Is it true what Shazia's just told me?' she asked.

'True about what?' I asked.

'That she's had FGM?'

'It is unfortunately,' I sighed. 'She's only just found out so it's been a huge shock for her.'

I could see Louisa was as horrified as I had been.

'I learnt about it when I did my nursery nurse training,' she said. 'Why would anyone do that to a child, Maggie?'

'I know, flower, it's awful. But you've got to remember that whatever we think, we can't project our feelings onto Shazia and criticise her family or their traditions in front of her.'

'But it's butchery,' she said.

I could only agree with her.

*

While all this was going on at home, the police had started an investigation after the consultant had reported it to them. Rachel rang to update me.

'The police called me today,' she said. 'They went round to talk to Shazia's parents about the FGM.'

'What did they say?' I asked.

'They were met with a wall of silence,' she replied. 'They refused to discuss it and wouldn't say anything at all.'

'The officer said unfortunately there's very little they can do, especially as Shazia doesn't remember it and it clearly happened years ago in a different country. It sounds like it's very hard to prosecute.'

She explained that although FGM has been a criminal offence in the UK since 1985, there had so far been no prosecutions in this country.

In the midst of all this, the time had come to have Shazia's eight-week review. This was a meeting where everyone involved in her care got together to talk about where we were at and what the long-term plan for her was going to be. I purposefully arranged it for a day when she was at Vicky's to give us all the time and space to meet at my house.

Becky and Rachel were coming along as well as Shazia's Independent Reviewing Officer (IRO) – a woman called Janet, who had been recently appointed and I hadn't met yet. An IRO was someone who worked at Social Services but wasn't directly involved in the case and who would make sure the child's needs were being met.

Janet was a larger than life woman with a bubbly personality and a huge mop of blonde curly hair. She was one of those people that you couldn't help but like.

Rachel was chairing the meeting.

'I'm honestly not sure where to start,' she sighed. 'So much has happened since the EPO was initially taken out.

'The reality is, Shazia's not going to be returning to her biological family,' said Rachel. 'She is telling us in no uncertain terms that she doesn't want to return home and there are serious safety concerns.

'We've had to deal with threatening behaviour, including threats from her brothers that they're going to kill her. Shazia has made allegations of physical violence, false imprisonment and forced marriage and last week we had the horrendous discovery that she'd suffered FGM as a child.'

I could see the look of absolute horror on Janet's face.

'Every day, Social Services staff have had to deal with her brothers coming in and being abusive and threatening when they won't tell them where she is, and they have to be removed by security,' she added. 'They've been cautioned by police now and have been told to stay away from the building.'

This was all news to me.

'Why didn't I know any of this?' I asked. 'Shouldn't you have told me?'

'Because it doesn't pose a direct risk to you or your home,' said Rachel. 'I knew you were already stressed and on edge, Maggie, and I didn't want to add to your worries. You didn't need to know because they clearly didn't know where Shazia was.'

In my mind it was important information and I was annoyed that she hadn't told me.

Rachel explained that Social Services had recently taken out a full care order on Shazia.

'As you'll see from the paperwork, Janet, and as I mentioned earlier, it's just been discovered that Shazia was subjected to FGM as a child,' Rachel told her.

'Horrific,' Janet sighed. 'How has she coped with that?'

'She's still very confused,' I replied. 'It's going to take her a long, long time to come to terms with it.'

Janet shook her head.

'So if she can't go back to her biological family, what's the thinking for her long term?'

'Because of the security issues and the threats from her family, I feel there's no other option than to move her out of the county,' said Rachel. 'It's truly the only way that she'll ever be safe.'

No matter how much it pained me to say so, I agreed with her. While she was living with me, Shazia would never be free.

'While she's living with me in this area, she can't have a life,' I told them. 'She needs to go back to school, she needs to mix with other kids and make friends. At the moment she's living in isolation.

'She's a lovely girl and I would love nothing more than to take her on long term, but I know in my heart that this can't happen. I think Shazia is starting to realise it too. She needs to feel safe.'

'I think it's clear that all of us feel that Shazia needs to be moved,' said Janet. 'Ideally she would be placed with a foster family with the same cultural background. I think because of the safety concerns with her family we need to seek police involvement and see if we can put together a multi-agency approach.'

At least we had all reached a decision about what needed to happen next, but I still came away from that meeting with a heavy heart. Shazia was going to be leaving and I wasn't sure how much more she was going to be able to cope with.

SIXTEEN

Extreme Measures

The noise of the vacuum cleaner drowned everything out so it was a good few minutes before I realised someone was frantically knocking on the front door.

Nervously I pulled back the net on the living-room window and peered out to see Rachel stood the doorstep. She gave me a cheerful wave.

'Sorry,' she said as I opened the door to her. 'I should have phoned. I was passing so I thought it was just as easy to drop in than ring.'

'No problem,' I smiled. 'I couldn't hear you over the hoover.'

'Where's Shazia?' she asked.

'She's upstairs,' I replied. 'Shall I call her down?'

'No, actually it's good that you and I can have a chat first,' she said.

Rachel explained that she had just come out of a meeting with the police to get their input about the long-term plans for Shazia.

'They were in total agreement with us that Shazia needs to be moved out of the county as soon as possible,' she said. 'They're taking the threats from her family very seriously. Although there's nothing that they can prosecute them for, at this stage they feel the risk to her safety is significant enough that they've agreed to move her under witness protection.'

'Really?' I said, surprised. 'I thought that was used to protect people in things like murder cases.'

'I think it can be used in any situation where the police feel that there's a big enough risk to that person's safety,' she replied.

'Wow,' I gasped. 'I vaguely understand what it is but I've never fostered a child who's been moved under witness protection before.'

'Neither have I,' she told me. 'But the police have talked me through it.'

She explained that witness protection would mean that Shazia would be given a completely new identity.

'Her name will be changed and she'll be moved to a new foster family in a new area,' she told me. 'Nobody will know her whereabouts except for myself and a couple of police officers. It costs the police a huge amount of money so they have to make sure that as few people as possible know that it's happening as they don't want to jeopardise it in any way. Your link worker has been informed but please don't tell anyone else.'

'What about Louisa?' I asked.

Rachel shook her head.

'I know it's tricky but it's not something that you can share with her,' she told me.

I knew it was going to be hard keeping something like that from someone I lived with.

'What sort of timescale are we looking at?' I asked her.

'The police want to try and sort something as soon as possible,' she told me. 'They're worried that because they've challenged the family about FGM, that that will incite her brothers even more.'

It was all so sudden and I was struggling to take in what Rachel was telling me. I knew Shazia had started to realise that she might have to move from my house for safety reasons, but witness protection was a whole different level. There would be nothing familiar that she could take with her from her old life, not even her name.

'The police will invent a bit of a back story for her and they'll chat to her about that when she's on the way to her new home,' said Rachel. 'They'll guide her through it and explain what she can or can't tell people.'

Like FGM, I knew this was something that Shazia was going to struggle to accept. She was barely starting to come to terms with what had happened to her and the long-term implications, and now we were dropping another bombshell on her.

'Do you mind calling her down so I can have a chat to her?' asked Rachel.

I went to fetch her from her bedroom.

'Rachel's downstairs,' I said. 'She'd like to talk to you.'

I could see her tense up. She'd come to dread Rachel coming round as she'd started to associate her visits with bad news. Sadly, most of the time lately she was right.

'I'll make us all a cup of tea in the kitchen,' I said, trying to steer us all away from the front room where only a few days previously we'd broken the news to Shazia about the FGM.

I put the kettle on while Rachel and Shazia sat down at the kitchen table.

'As Maggie's probably told you, we've been doing lots of talking about what might be best for you long term,' she told her.

'I know what you're going to say,' she sighed. 'I have to move, don't I?'

Rachel nodded sympathetically.

'Both the police and Social Services want you to be as safe as possible and we both agree that we need to move you to a different foster family in a new area,' she explained.

'But I am in a new area,' replied Shazia. 'Maggie lives in a different place to my family.'

'I don't think this is far away enough, sweetie,' I said. 'We still use the same parks, shops and hospital as members of your family so there's always a risk of us bumping into someone.'

'Maggie's right,' added Rachel. 'We feel it needs to be in a different county for you to be truly safe. The police know all about your brothers and the threats they've made, as well as their attempt to pull you into the car, and they're so concerned about your safety that they're going to give you something called witness protection. Have you heard of it?'

Shazia shook her head.

'What does it mean?' she asked, looking worried.

'It means that the police will be involved in helping you move. To make sure that your family can never ever find you, they'll give you a new name and you'll be moved to live with a new family in a new town,' explained Rachel.

'A new name?' she gasped. 'So I won't be called Shazia any more?'

'That's right,' she replied. 'And you'll have a new surname too.'

'But if I'm not called Shazia, what will I be called?' she asked, looking bewildered. 'Do you know what my new name will be, Maggie?'

I sat down at the table.

'I don't know, lovey,' I told her. 'And I'm afraid I won't be allowed to know either. I won't be told anything about what you're called or where you've gone,' I explained. 'The only people who will have that information are Rachel and probably a couple of police officers and your new foster family.'

'But you and Louisa will be able to visit me, won't you?' she asked, her voice tinged with desperation. 'And Zeena. Zeena will be able to come and see me won't she?'

My heart broke for her as I shook my head.

'I'm so sorry, lovey,' I said, putting a comforting hand on her shoulder. 'In order to protect you, you can't keep in touch with anyone from your old life. Our contact with you will have to end. It's too risky. Your brothers might recognise me and follow me and then they will know where you are.'

Shazia looked up at me, aghast, her eyes wide with fear.

'Maggie's right,' nodded Rachel. 'It means no letters or phone calls or visits. No one must know where you are or that your name used to be Shazia Bains.'

'But who's my new family going to be?' she asked. 'When can I meet them?'

'I'm in touch with lots of other Social Services around the country so I'm going to find your new family,' Rachel told her. 'But I'm afraid you won't be able to meet them until the day you go and live with them.'

I could see the shock on Shazia's face and she looked like she was going to burst into tears. I think in her heart she had always known that she would have to move on eventually, but to sever contact with her past completely was a concept that would have been hard for any adult to cope with, never mind a child.

I really felt for her. She was so vulnerable, and she'd been through so much, and now we were telling her that everything she'd ever known was going to change, even down to her name. Normally when children are moved on, there's a settling in period and they get to visit their new family a few times before moving in. In this case, Shazia wouldn't meet them until she was literally standing on their doorstep with her suitcase. But I knew it was the only way to make sure that she couldn't be tracked down.

My heart was torn. I wanted her to be safe and have a life but this seemed so extreme. It was so final somehow.

Rachel quickly finished her tea.

'I'm so sorry, but I have to go,' she said. 'I have to get back to the office. Shazia, if you have any questions, I'm sure Maggie will be able to answer them.

'I'll be in touch,' she told me on her way out.

Talk about dropping a bombshell and then leaving. When I went back into the kitchen, Shazia looked absolutely lost and petrified.

'What if I don't like the foster family they send me to?' she asked meekly. 'What if I hate my new name?'

I sat down next to her and took hold of her hand.

'Even though you can't meet them before you move, Rachel will,' I told her, desperately wanting to reassure her. 'She's going to make sure that she picks a lovely family for you to go and live with who will really look after you. And she'll pick a family that reflects your heritage too so you'll feel comfortable culturally.'

'But what if they're strict like my dad and my brothers?' she asked. 'What if they want to me to go to Pakistan and get married too?'

'Whoever it will be will have had to go through a long, rigorous process in order to become foster carers,' I explained gently. 'They'll have been vetted by Social Services. And while it's fine for everyone to have their own beliefs, they certainly won't be allowed to force you into getting married.'

Shazia still looked terrified.

'No,' she said firmly, letting go of my hand and pushing it away. 'I'm staying here with you and not doing this witness thing. You can't make me go.'

'Shazia, I know it's so hard and scary for you, but believe me when I tell you that there is no other way if you want to have a normal life,' I told her. 'If you truly want to be free and not spend the rest of your life living in fear from your family, then this is your only option.

'You're not going to have to do this on your own. You'll have the support of your new family and the police and Social Services. Rachel will make sure that you continue to have counselling.'

'With Aisha?' she asked.

'It probably won't be with Aisha,' I said sadly. 'But she'll find you a new counsellor who you can talk everything through with and you'll be able to see a new consultant to talk about dealing with the FGM.'

She looked shell-shocked.

'I know it's a lot to take in, sweetie,' I soothed. 'I don't want to see you go either but this is the only way. You deserve a life and you deserve to be happy.'

'But why can't I stay here with you and Louisa?' she asked, her eyes filling with tears. 'My family don't know where I am. They haven't come round.'

'I know, lovey, but we can't go out anywhere in case we bump into them,' I said. 'You can't go to school or see your friends. We have to drive for two hours if we even want go shopping. You can't live like that forever.'

I didn't say it to her as I didn't want to hurt her feelings, but I knew I couldn't live like this in the long term either.

She looked up at me, her face streaked with tears.

'Maggie, couldn't you and Louisa just move house so I can carry on living with you and then we'd all be safe?'

I leant over and gave her a hug.

'Sweetheart, I wish I could but it's not as easy as that, I'm afraid,' I told her. 'My life is here. This is where my fostering agency is and Graham and my friends. Besides, it costs a lot of money to move house and I couldn't afford it.'

I could totally understand why she was so frightened.

'I know this feels scary. The unknown always is, but you have to realise this is being done for all the right reasons. It has to be like this to keep you safe. There is no other option and you have to put your trust in Rachel and the police.

'You deserve to have a life,' I told her. 'You deserve to be able to go to school or to the cinema, to be able to go out and meet friends and not be worried about being hurt or threatened. You need to be somewhere you know that you are safe instead of being trapped here in these four walls with me.'

'When will I have to go?' she asked sadly.

'I know the police would like to get you out of the area as soon as possible,' I said. 'As soon as Rachel knows more, she'll let us know.'

Rachel had already warned me that it could happen in a matter of days and the most we would get is a few hours' notice. They'd literally ring me up one morning and tell me that today was the day Shazia had to leave.

I didn't want to tell Shazia that, though. I didn't want her to have to live with the anxiety of waking up every morning and wondering if today was going to be the day that we got the call.

It would be a shock for us both when it happened, but at least it would give her less time to dwell on it and wind herself up.

Later that afternoon Becky rang me.

'I've just spoken to Rachel and she explained what's happening with Shazia,' she said. 'How are you feeling about it?'

'To be honest it's a big shock,' I told her. 'I've never done a handover like this before. I'm not sure how to prepare Shazia or even myself.

'It feels so unsettling because I don't know when she's leaving,' I added. 'And how on earth do I reassure her if I know nothing about where she's going?'

'I'm afraid I'm not much help because I've never had experience of a child going into witness protection either,' she sighed. 'Just do the best you can, Maggie.'

But would my best be good enough?

*

As each day passed, I could see the thought of leaving was preying on Shazia's mind. It was understandable. I felt on edge too and I jumped every time my phone rang, wondering if this was the call. On a practical level, I knew it might take a while for Rachel to find a suitable foster family that shared Shazia's heritage. But nevertheless I knew we needed to be prepared as it could happen at any time.

'Do you want to go upstairs and start sorting through your things?' I asked her one day.

She'd come with nothing but a tatty old nightdress she'd been wearing when she escaped out of the window that day, so she didn't have many belongings. She didn't have toys and games like a younger child, but I'd bought her books and clothes and a few little nick-nacks for her room that would need sorting out.

She'd been up there for ten minutes when I went to check on her. I found her sat on the floor clutching a carrier bag to her chest.

She looked up as I came in.

'I found this in the wardrobe,' she said.

'What is it?' I asked.

She opened the bag and pulled out a couple of shalwar kameez. They were the ones her parents had sent when she had first been taken into care all those months ago.

She tenderly stroked the material, then she clasped one of them in her hands, put it over her nose and mouth and breathed in.

'They smell like home,' she said sadly.

Tears streamed down her face as the realisation hit her that she didn't have a home or a family any more.

'I'm never going to see my mum again, am I?' she sobbed.

I shook my head.

'I'm so, so sorry,' I told her.

I went and sat next to her on the floor.

'Do you miss her?' I asked.

'All the time,' she nodded. 'I want to stop loving her after everything that's happened but I can't.'

It was such a hard mix of emotions for her to deal with. She was upset and bitter that her mother had deceived her, but at the same time she was bereft at the thought of never seeing her again. Even though her family had put her through so much, they were still her family and she was grieving for the fact that she would never see them again.

'Maybe I should have just done what they wanted and gone to Pakistan,' she sobbed. 'Maybe getting married would have been easier than this.'

'You're still a child,' I told her. 'Did you really want to get married? Do you really feel like you're ready to be someone's wife?'

She shook her head.

She handed me the carrier bag of her old clothes.

'Throw them away,' she told me defiantly. 'I don't want them any more.'

She'd been let down by the people who were supposed to love and protect her the most and I knew that it was going to take her a very long time to even begin to come to terms with that.

SEVENTEEN

The Call

We were living life in a state of limbo. A week had passed since Rachel had told me about Shazia being moved under police protection, but so far it hadn't happened.

It was now the school summer holidays and Glynis the tutor wasn't coming any more, so our days under house arrest seemed even longer. It felt like we were spending each day waiting for the call that was going to change Shazia's life forever.

I couldn't help but feel like I was letting her down because I couldn't give her a proper goodbye. We couldn't tell anyone she was going and we didn't know when it was going to be. I normally made a memory box for every child who I'd fostered for more than a few weeks, but I couldn't even do that for Shazia. Rachel had warned us the less she took with her from her old life, the better, and photographs were a definite no-no.

I could see that Shazia was unsettled and scared about what was about to happen. She wasn't sleeping properly and at mealtimes she just picked at her food listlessly. She looked pale and withdrawn, and I knew there was nothing I could do to make things easier. It was the unknown for both of us and I was at a loss to know how best to prepare or reassure her about what was going to happen.

Louisa had noticed Shazia's low mood and began to suspect there was something going on.

'What's wrong with Shazia?' she asked me one night when she was in bed. 'She's so quiet.'

'She's got a lot to think about at the moment,' I told her. 'Rachel has started talking to her about the fact that she probably can't live here permanently because it isn't safe for her.'

'Oh, you mean she might have to move to another foster home?' she asked. 'Yeah, I suppose you're right.'

'I'm just letting her get her head around it really,' I replied.

While I wasn't technically lying to Louisa, I felt guilty that I wasn't able to tell her the whole truth. But I knew my hands were tied and I couldn't. Even when Graham rang up to see how I was, I couldn't mention anything.

'Are you alright, Maggie?' he asked.

'Yes, why?' I replied distractedly.

'Do you never check your voicemail? I must have left at least three messages for you over the past week.'

'I'm so sorry,' I told him. 'There's a lot going on at home right now. I'll tell you more about it when I see you.'

'When *am* I going to get to see you?' he asked.

'Hopefully things will be a bit easier in a few weeks,' I told him. 'I promise I'll give you a ring.'

For the foreseeable future I knew I needed to focus on Shazia, but because there was very little I could say to reassure her, I felt utterly helpless. I couldn't talk to Shazia about her new family and what pets they had or what colour her new bedroom was painted or about the other children living in the house. I couldn't make any of the preparations that I normally did with a child who was moving on because I didn't know anything about her new family and I never would. It was a painful, horrible situation for her to be in.

However, I think that as adults we often try to talk to children too much. I've learnt over the years that you've got to give children the space to absorb things in their own time. Sometimes it's just about being there and giving them lots of physical contact. So if Shazia was sitting at the kitchen table and I could see that she was deep in thought or looking upset, I would put a hand on her shoulder or give her a gentle kiss on the top of her head. Simple little gestures like that would help to comfort her and let her know that I was there if she needed me.

'Is there anything that you'd like to do before you go?' I asked Shazia one morning in a desperate bid to cheer her up.

'Yes, I want to see Zeena,' she said decisively. 'I'd like to see her one last time so I can say goodbye.'

'Do you think I could do that, Maggie?'

Her eyes shone with excitement.

'I honestly don't know, flower,' I told her. 'So try not to get your hopes up until I've run it by Rachel.'

I gave her a ring that morning.

'I don't think that's a good idea,' said Rachel when I told her what Shazia had asked. 'We know her brothers know where Zeena lives.'

'What if I took the girls shopping to another city a couple of hours away?' I suggested. 'We could see if Naz could drop

Zeena off at a service station on the motorway and I could pick her up and drop her off there.'

It would take a lot of organising but I was determined to make it happen.

'OK,' sighed Rachel when she sensed I wasn't going to give up on the idea without a fight. 'But on one condition. Shazia can't mention anything to Zeena about witness protection or having to leave the area. She can't tell her that this is the last time that she's going to see her. In fact, it's best if she doesn't mention anything about moving foster carers at all.'

'I'll make sure I drum that into her,' I said. 'She's going to be so pleased.'

I texted Naz and thankfully she agreed to the shopping trip. Shazia looked so happy when I told her. It made me realise how long it had been since I'd seen her smile. A couple of days later we had a handover at the service station.

'I'll give you a ring when we're on our way back and we'll meet you here,' I told Naz.

'OK,' she said, a worried look on her face. 'Take care.'

'It will be fine,' I reassured her. 'We're deliberately going miles away so we've got no chance of bumping into any of Shazia's family.'

When the girls were reunited they fell into each other's arms. They spent the rest of the journey gossiping about friends and what had been happening at school.

'I've missed you so much, Shaz,' Zeena told her. 'It's so boring without you. Do you think you'll be able to come back to school in September?'

'Oh-er maybe,' said Shazia hesitantly, while giving me a look of pure panic.

'What does everyone fancy for lunch then?' I said, quickly changing the subject.

One meal at Café Rouge and several shops later, the girls were having a great time. I lurked behind them the whole time, looking around us nervously, even though I knew the chances of us bumping into anyone who knew Shazia were minimal.

Shazia had some pocket money that she'd saved up during her time with me and she spotted something in the window of a jewellery shop.

It was pair of silver necklaces that formed a heart shape with 'Besties' written in the middle of it. The heart split in two and each necklace had half of the heart on it.

'I'm going to get these for us,' Shazia told Zeena, excitedly.

'Are you sure?' she gasped. 'It's gorgeous.'

I could see Shazia was struggling to hold back the tears as she fastened Zeena's necklace around her neck.

'Besties forever,' smiled Zeena. 'Thank you so much. I love it.'

As our day out drew to a close, I could see that Shazia looked drawn and tired. This was so hard for her.

'We've got to head back, girls,' I told them. 'I'll send Naz a text letting her know we're on our way.'

As I pulled into the service station to drop Zeena off, I could see Shazia's face crumple at the sight of Naz's car.

'I'm afraid it's time to say goodbye now,' I told her gently.

The girls gave each other a hug. Shazia clung onto her friend for dear life as she said goodbye. Even I struggled to hold back the tears, knowing that it would be the last time the girls would ever see each other.

'I love you, Zee,' she told her. 'You've been the best friend anyone could possibly have.'

'You're being really soppy today,' Zeena laughed, looking surprised. 'You must have really missed me. I'll see you soon when everything gets back to normal,' she said cheerfully as she got out of the car.

I walked Zeena over to where Naz was waiting. When I got back to the car and opened the driver's door, all I could hear was sobbing. Shazia was curled up in a ball on the back seat in floods of tears.

I got out and climbed into the back with her and she slumped into my arms.

'I can't believe I'll never see her again,' she whimpered. 'It's not fair, Maggie. It's just not fair.'

'I know this is really difficult for you,' I soothed. 'But there is no other way. You'll make new friends.'

'I don't want new friends,' she howled. 'I want Zee.'

All I could do was hold her while she sobbed her little heart out. It was heart-wrenching to witness and I felt my eyes filling with tears too. I stayed like that for ages, cuddling her until her tears ran dry. I felt helpless seeing her huge sense of loss and knowing that there was absolutely nothing that I could do or say to make it any better. How much pain could one little girl take?

By the time we got back I could see that Shazia was exhausted. It was all starting to hit home what being in witness protection really meant. That night I went up to see her before she went to sleep.

'It's been such a hard day for you,' I sighed. 'How are you doing?'

She shrugged. 'I just feel really, really sad.

'Maggie, you know how Rachel let me see Zeena? Do you think she'd let me see my mum before I go? Not my brothers or my dad. Just my mum.'

'I'm sorry, sweetie,' I told her. 'But Rachel and the police would never allow that. What if she told your brothers where you were going to be? It would put your mum in a difficult position and be way too much of a risk to you.'

I understood why she wanted to see her mum. She had so many unanswered questions and she desperately wanted some sort of closure.

'Will anyone tell my family that I'm going?' she asked.

I explained that Social Services would have notified them when a full care order had been taken out to say that she was now in the care system permanently.

'Rachel will probably write to them after you've moved telling them that you've left the area indefinitely.'

That was all they'd ever be allowed to know.

A couple of days later we woke up to torrential rain.

'Typical British summer weather,' I sighed at the thought of another long day in the house stretching out before us. 'Do you fancy watching a DVD? Or we could do a bit of baking?'

'Again,' sighed Shazia. 'I'm so bored of that.'

She had just gone upstairs for a shower when my mobile rang. Rachel's number flashed up on the screen. There was no polite greeting and she got straight to the point.

'Maggie, we're going to move Shazia today,' she told me matter of factly. 'I'll be round at one o'clock to pick her up so can you please make sure that she's ready.'

'Today?' I gasped. 'One o'clock? But that's in three hours.'

Even though I knew this was going to happen at some point, it was still a shock.

'I know it's sudden but this is the way the police have to do things,' she told me. 'An officer called DC Kiran Gupta will come round shortly before I arrive just to double-check what Shazia's taking with her. She'll then drive us both to the new location.'

'OK,' I told her, shakily. 'I'll make sure she's ready.'

I hung up and paced up and down the kitchen, my stomach churning with nerves. First of all, I needed to tell Shazia what was happening.

I waited until she'd had her shower and come back downstairs. Inside I felt panicked, but I wanted to keep calm for her. I obviously didn't hide my feelings very well, though.

'What is it, Maggie?' she asked the minute she saw my face. 'What's happened?'

'Rachel has just called,' I told her. 'You're going to be moving today.'

Her mouth gaped open with shock.

'What, I'm going today?' she gasped. 'Now?'

'Yes,' I told her. 'Rachel will be coming round in a few hours.'

'But I can't go today,' she exclaimed, looking stricken. 'I haven't packed my things or said bye to Louisa or anything.'

'Your things are pretty much sorted,' I reminded her. 'Rachel said to bring as little as possible.'

'But when am I going? Who's going to take me? How long will it take to get there?' she babbled.

'Sweetie, I know this is a shock but try and stay calm,' I told her gently. 'I don't know how long it's going to take because I don't know where you're going.

'You're not going to be on your own. Rachel's going to come with you as well as a police officer, so they will talk you through everything in the car. She's going to come round here at one o'clock to collect you.'

'One?' she sighed. 'But that's so soon. What about lunch?'

'I'll make up a packed lunch and you can eat it in the car,' I told her.

I could see she was terrified.

I went over and hugged her tightly.

'I know it's scary but you're going to be absolutely fine, I promise,' I told her. 'It's going to be OK.'

'What if I say no?' she asked. 'What if I say I don't want to go?'

'Shazia, remember, we talked about this the other week,' I told her. 'I'm afraid it's your only option.

'Think of it as an adventure,' I continued, trying to be positive. 'By the end of today you'll have met your new foster family and you'll know your new name.'

'I don't want a new name,' she sobbed. 'I just want to watch a DVD and do baking.'

'An hour ago baking was the last thing you wanted to do,' I smiled, giving the top of her head a kiss.

'Come on, we'd better go upstairs and sort your things out,' I told her gently.

I knew that she couldn't take anything with her name on, like school books or diaries or anything familiar like her school bag.

'What about these?' she asked, showing me a strip of little passport photos of her and Zeena taken in a photo booth. They were grinning, sticking their tongues out and doing the 'peace' sign.

'I'm sorry lovey, but you can't take them,' I told her reluctantly.

She looked at them sadly before handing them over to me.

It was strange for me too having her leave in such a secretive, sudden way. It had to be the most bizarre goodbye that I'd had in my entire fostering career.

I went and sat down next to Shazia on the bed.

'Before you go I wanted to give you this,' I said, handing her a small blue box that I fished out of the pocket of my trousers. She opened it up to reveal a gold chain bracelet with a delicate little heart charm on it.

'It's to show you that even though you're not with me any more, I'll always carry you in my heart,' I told her. 'Whenever you're missing us or you're feeling scared or upset, you can hold this little heart in your hand, close your eyes and know that I'm thinking of you.'

'Really?' she asked, staring up at me. 'Will you really think of me, Maggie?'

'Of course I will,' I smiled. 'I will think of you when I try and make samosas and I can't get them to stick together and they all keep falling apart. And I'll think of you whenever Louisa and I play Kerplunk or Monopoly and we'll remember how you always used to beat us.

'There are lots of times when I'll think of you.'

Suddenly there was a knock at the front door. Shazia looked up at me, her eyes filled with fear.

'I'd better go and see who that is,' I said.

A small Asian woman in her forties was stood there in jeans and a t-shirt. She showed me her ID and I unhooked the chain.

'DC Gupta,' she smiled. 'Hopefully Rachel told you I was coming.'

'Yes, sorry,' I said. 'You confused me because you weren't in uniform.'

'It's safer that way and we'll take her in an unmarked car,' she told me.

I took her upstairs to meet Shazia.

'Shazia, this is DC Gupta. She's a police officer and she's going to be taking you to your new foster placement.'

Shazia eyed her up suspiciously.

'I thought Rachel was taking me,' she said.

'She is,' she told her. 'She'll be here soon.'

DC Gupta was very gentle and kind and she patiently answered Shazia's questions.

'Do you know what my new name is?' she asked her. 'Do you know where we're going?'

'We'll talk about that in the car,' she told her.

In a weird way, it felt like I'd done something wrong as I wasn't allowed to know anything about Shazia's new life.

Rachel arrived fifteen minutes later.

'How's she doing?' she asked.

I shrugged.

'She's pretty terrified, but hopefully you can talk her though it. What shall I do with the things that she's not allowed to take?' I asked.

'You need to get rid of them as soon as you can,' she replied. 'I would either burn them or shred them just to be on the safe side.'

'I know you can't tell me much, but will you let me know how it went and how Shazia is?' I asked her.

'Of course,' she said. 'I'm going to stay in the area with her for a couple of days to make sure that she's happy and settled. When I'm back in the office later this week I'll give you a call.'

'Thank you,' I said. 'I'd really appreciate that.'

I knew it would be preying on my mind.

Just then, Shazia came downstairs with DC Gupta clutching a small holdall. She looked so scared and vulnerable. I wrapped my arms around her and drew her to me.

'You will be fine,' I whispered, stroking her hair.

'All set?' asked Rachel. She looked at her watch. 'We'd best be getting on the road.'

Shazia held up her bag.

'She wouldn't let me take hardly anything,' she sighed.

'Don't worry, your new foster family will be able to sort you out with some clothes when you get there,' Rachel reassured her.

The time had come to say goodbye. Every goodbye I'd ever had with a child had always been so carefully managed. This was the complete opposite – it was rushed and sudden and I knew there was nothing I could do or say that could take away Shazia's fear.

'I'm going to miss you,' I told her, giving her another huge hug. 'And I know Louisa will too.'

'Will you say bye to her for me?' she asked.

I nodded.

'Thank you for being kind to me, Maggie,' she said. 'I'll never forget you.'

Her eyes were filled with fear and sadness.

'It's going to be OK,' I told her.

'You're free, Shazia. You're free to live your life the way you want to live it, so make the most of it.'

As true as that was, we both knew that her freedom had come at a price.

'I'll give you a call, Maggie,' Rachel told me.

I watched as the three of them walked out to the ordinary-looking car parked outside. As Shazia got into the back, she stopped and turned to me. She held up her wrist to show me that she was wearing her new bracelet and I smiled. As the car engine started, she looked straight ahead and didn't turn around.

I watched them drive away until the car disappeared off into the distance.

I closed the front door and waited for the tears to flow like they often did when a child had just left and I was out of their sight. However, this time I couldn't cry, I just felt numb.

One minute Shazia was here, the next she was gone. It felt so strange. With a heavy heart I cleared away her empty cereal bowl and the half-drunk glass of orange juice that were still on the kitchen table.

I suddenly felt exhausted. Since Rachel had phoned that morning the adrenalin had been pumping while I'd got Shazia ready to leave, but now I just felt drained.

Even though I felt tired I knew I didn't want to stay in the house. I was sick to death of these four walls. The reality was, now Shazia was gone I didn't have to stay inside any more. It was still raining outside but I didn't care. I left the house and just walked and walked, feeling the rain lash against my face, making me feel alive.

I felt guilty but in a way I also felt relieved. Now Shazia had gone I didn't have to flinch every time there was a knock at the door or constantly be checking for the nearest emergency exit. I was free too.

The fresh air helped to clear my head and I realised I'd been walking for over an hour when I sat down on a bench outside a parade of shops. I thought about Shazia. Where was she now? How was she doing? How long until she got to her new home? I remembered her frightened little face as she'd climbed into the police car and at last, the tears started to flow. Once they'd started, I couldn't stop and I sat there in the rain sobbing my heart out.

EIGHTEEN

Goodbye to the Past

Tears were still streaming down my face when I felt my mobile phone ringing in my jacket pocket.

It was Becky.

'I've just had a text from Rachel to say that Shazia has gone,' she said. 'How are you doing?'

'Well at the moment I'm sat on a bench in the rain crying,' I told her.

'Oh no,' she gasped. 'Are you OK, Maggie?'

'I'll be fine,' I sniffed, reaching for a tissue from my bag. 'I just feel a bit sad that's all. It was all so sudden, and she looked so frightened, Becky.'

'She'll have lots of support and help to settle in,' she reassured me. 'She won't be on her own and she'll continue with counselling.'

'I know,' I sighed. 'It just felt strange sending her off into the unknown. I felt like I hadn't done my job properly somehow. She was asking the police officer lots of questions and she couldn't answer them because I was there and I wasn't allowed to know the information. It made me feel like I'd done something wrong.'

'You know you can talk to me about it any time,' she told me. 'My door is always open.'

'Thanks, Becky,' I said. 'It all feels a bit raw at the moment.'

By the time I'd walked back home again, I was shattered and soaked through to my skin. But I knew I needed to do what Rachel had asked and get rid of Shazia's things straightaway. The rain had stopped now so I went outside and lit a bonfire in the fire bin at the bottom of the garden. As the flames licked the outside of the metal, I got the pile of school books, jotters and photographs and one by one threw them into the flames.

It felt so strange watching all the remnants from Shazia's old life crackle and burn into ashes. Even the shalwar kameez that she had brought from home had to be destroyed.

Goodbye Shazia, I thought to myself as I watched the material disappear into the orange glow.

I realised that she would have her new name by now so Shazia didn't officially exist any more.

Finally I came to the strip of passport photos of Shazia and Zeena. I was about to throw them into the fire too when something stopped me.

'Besties forever,' I smiled to myself as I looked at their grinning faces. They looked so happy and carefree in the pictures, I couldn't bring myself to burn them. Instead, I tucked them into the pocket of my jeans. I didn't think I was breaking any rules by keeping them.

I headed back inside and went into the dining room. One alcove of the room was filled with shelves and on those shelves was album upon album of photographs of all of the hundreds of children that I had fostered over the years.

I opened the most recent album that was half full and smiled at the picture of a baby-faced Michael when he first arrived with me and one I'd taken on his first birthday. I got the strip of passport photos out of my pocket, peeled back the plastic and placed them in there. Shazia was part of the story of my fostering and she deserved to be in my album. From time to time I'd get the photo albums out and flick through them and I always felt an overwhelming sense of satisfaction and pride. I wanted to open it years later and see Shazia's smiling face and remember everything that she had gone through and how brave she'd been. For three months she had been part of my family and I wanted a record of that. It was strange thinking that perhaps the only place the old Shazia existed in the world now was inside the pages of my photo album.

I'd just walked back into the kitchen to make a cup of tea when Louisa came in from work.

'Where's Shazia?' she asked as she put her keys down on the table.

'She's gone,' I said quietly.

'Gone where?' she asked, puzzled. 'I thought she wasn't allowed out on her own any more.'

'No, I'm afraid she's gone for good, lovey,' I told her. 'She was moved to a new foster family out of the county this afternoon.'

'What?' she gasped. 'How come?'

I explained how she'd had to be moved under police protection and that I hadn't been allowed to tell anyone. It wasn't often that Louisa lost her temper, but I could see that she was angry and upset.

'I'm part of this family and I live with you, so why did you lie to me?' she yelled, her eyes filled with tears.

'I didn't lie,' I told her calmly. 'I wasn't able to give you all the information because I wasn't allowed to.'

'In all the placements you've ever had, it's never been like this before,' she replied. 'You've always told me the truth and I've always been able to say goodbye. If I'd known I could have said bye to her this morning.'

'This time I couldn't tell you what was happening because I was sworn to secrecy,' I explained. 'I desperately wanted to, but I didn't want to risk jeopardising the whole thing. If I'd told you you might have mentioned it to Charlie who might have mentioned it to someone else and I couldn't take that risk.

'I didn't even know she was going myself until a couple of hours before. Rachel literally phoned me at 11 this morning and said Shazia had to leave this afternoon, so it was a shock for me too.'

'I'm sorry, Maggie,' she sighed. 'It's just so sudden. She was a nice girl. I would have liked to have said goodbye to her.'

'I know,' I replied. 'I'm sorry. I wish things could have been different, but it had to be this way.'

Shazia leaving had left us both feeling a huge sense of loss. Normally when I moved a child to a new family I had contact with them. I'd see the house they were going to live in and get a glimpse of the life they were going to have. With Shazia I knew nothing. Her name had been changed so we didn't even know what she was called.

Like Louisa, I was struggling to process it too. That night I felt too drained to cook so I ordered a pizza and Louisa and I ate it in front of the TV.

By 9 o'clock I was ready for bed. I walked into my bedroom and pulled back the covers to find three notes on my pillow. I recognised Shazia's handwriting straightaway. One said 'Maggie', one said 'Mum' and the other one was addressed to 'Zeena'.

With trembling hands, I unfolded the piece of paper that was addressed to me.

Thank you for everything Maggie. I loved being at your house with you and Louisa and I will miss you loads. Please pass these letters on. I didn't want the police or Rachel to see them in case they wouldn't let me. Shazia xx

Curiousity got the better of me and I knew I had to read the other two notes. They weren't in envelopes and I knew I'd have to look at them anyway, as Rachel would want to know what they said so she could judge whether it was OK to pass them on.

I read Zeena's first.

Zee, you won't see me ever again. Sorry I couldn't tell you the other day. I've had to move somewhere far away and I'm not allowed to contact anyone from my old life. I'll miss you so much. Thank you for being my friend.

Shaz xxx

The last and longest note was to her mum.

Dear Mum, I wanted to tell you before I went away that even though I can't see you, I still think about you. I miss making samosas with you and you doing my hair and telling me stories. I'm sorry I didn't want to go to Pakistan but I was frightened about getting married. I'm still feeling sad and confused about the things that have happened to me. I'm trying to understand why you did them. Maggie says maybe you thought you were doing your best for me so that's what I'm trying to believe. I don't miss Adil and Dev and all the horrible things they said and did to me. But I like to think that you didn't know they were doing them. It will feel strange going to live with a new family. I still can't believe I will never see you again but I wanted you to know that I still love you and I will miss you always. I hope you still love me too.

Love from your daughter, Shazia xxx

My heart broke reading her desperate words and by the time I got to the end, I was sobbing my heart out.

My tears were for Shazia and what she'd lost. She had so many questions that would never be answered now and I hoped that in some small way she would be able to move on with her new family and eventually find some sort of closure.

I slept heavily that night. By the time I woke up the next morning, Louisa had already gone to work and the house was eerily quiet. I was eating my breakfast when Rachel rang.

'I'm just calling to let you know that it all went OK yesterday,' she told me.

'How's Shazia?' I asked.

'It's been hard for her but she had a good first night and she seems to like her new family.'

'Oh I'm relieved,' I said. 'I've been thinking about her.'

'I'm afraid I won't be able to give you any more updates,' said Rachel. 'From tomorrow, the case has been transferred to the local Social Services where she lives now so she'll have a new social worker.'

It was so final.

'Before you go, Rachel, I need to talk to you about something else,' I told her. 'Shazia left a couple of notes that she wanted me to pass onto Zeena and her mum.'

'What did they say?' she asked.

I read them to her over the phone and once again, I felt myself filling up at her anguished words.

'They're heartbreaking,' sighed Rachel. 'But I'm so sorry, Maggie, we can't risk passing these on. We don't want to give Zeena or her family any more information about where she is and what's happened to her. We don't want to jeopardise all the hard work it's taken to move her.'

'Are you sure?' I asked.

I felt like I was letting Shazia down by not passing them on but equally I understood why.

'I'm sure,' she told me firmly.

The following afternoon I had a bit of light relief in the form of a visit to see Michael and Kerry. Louisa came with me and as we walked up the stairs towards their first floor flat, I could see Michael standing at the window.

'There he is!' squealed Louisa and we both laughed as he pressed his mouth against the pane and blew raspberries on the glass.

Kerry looked tired but happy as she opened the door and we both gave her a hug.

'Where's Shazia?' she asked. 'I thought you'd be bringing her.'

Louisa and I exchanged glances.

'Oh, she's moved on to a new foster home now,' I told her vaguely.

'That's a shame,' she said. 'She seemed like a nice girl.'

'She was,' I nodded, swallowing the lump in my throat.

Michael was as full of beans as ever as he ran around the living room. He showed Louisa all his toys while I went into the kitchen with Kerry to make a cup of tea.

'How are you doing?' I asked her.

'I can't deny it's been tough,' she sighed. 'I'm still on my medication and Michael is hard work but I'm coping.

'I love him so much, Maggie,' she grinned. 'He makes me smile every day and he's the reason I get out of bed every morning.'

'That's lovely to hear,' I said.

I was so proud of her. As we were talking, Michael ran into the kitchen and tripped over one of his toys and fell onto the floor with a thud.

'Oh baby, did you hurt yourself?' I cooed.

I picked him up but he struggled in my arms.

'Mum-mum-mum,' he shouted leaning over towards Kerry and putting his arms out to her.

'I was hoping to sneak in a cuddle but I think he wants his mummy,' I smiled, genuinely delighted to see the strong bond that the pair of them had.

Louisa and I left with a big smile on our faces. It was lovely to see how happy and settled Michael was and going to visit them had given me a much-needed boost after the sadness of the past few days.

Shazia was still very much on my mind though and I knew she would be for a long time. I took it easy over the next few days. I went for long walks, had baths, met Graham for dinner and even finished reading a whole book. It felt very self-indulgent, but slowly I began to feel less exhausted.

A week after Shazia had left, my phone rang one morning.

It was a withheld number that flashed up on the screen so I couldn't tell who it was.

'Hello,' I answered.

'Maggie?' said a familiar voice. 'Is that really you?'

'Shazia!' I gasped. 'Are you alright?'

'I know I shouldn't be ringing you, but I was missing you and I just wanted to hear your voice,' she told me. 'And I needed to tell you something.'

'What is it?' I asked.

'I wanted to say that I think everything's going to be OK and my new family seem nice. I wanted you to know because I knew that you'd be worried about me.'

'I'm so, so glad,' I sighed. 'And you're right: you've been on my mind constantly.'

'This is the last time I'm ever going to speak to you, isn't it?' she asked sadly.

'I'm afraid it is, sweetie,' I said. 'It has to be. But thank you so much for calling me.'

'I miss you, Maggie,' she whispered.

'I miss you too,' I said.

And just like that, she was gone.

I was so pleased to have heard from her, but I knew it was against the rules and I was going to have to tell Rachel that she'd called.

'She did what?' she ranted when I rang. 'Did she not listen to a word that me or the police said?'

'Did she tell you where she was and what her new name was?' she asked anxiously.

'No, not a thing,' I said. 'And she said she was ringing from a phone box so it was an unknown number.'

'It should be OK then,' she told me. 'But I'll make sure her new social worker has a stern word with her.'

I knew it was against the rules, but deep down I was glad that Shazia had rung. It had reassured me hearing her voice.

She deserved to be happy and I desperately wanted her to have her freedom. I wanted her to be able to live her life the way she wanted to and love whom she wanted to without any pressures or fears.

I'd done what I could for Shazia, but I knew it was going to take years for her to come to terms both physically and emotionally with what had happened with her biological family. The hardest part for me to come to terms with was the knowledge that I would never hear from her again. There was nothing I loved more than hearing updates from children that I'd fostered, sometimes years after they'd left.

Even if it was just a card at Christmas, a text out of the blue or a Facebook message, I liked to hear how they were getting on. With Shazia, I knew that was it. I didn't know her name or where she was. It was final. I would never hear anything about her again. I'd never know how she'd settled with her new family or how she got on in her GSCEs.

But wherever she is now, many years later, all I can do is hope that she's happy and safe and she's enjoying the freedom that she was forced to give up everything for.

Later that afternoon I phoned Becky.

'You sound a bit brighter, Maggie,' she told me.

'I am,' I replied. 'In fact I'm ringing to see if you can put me back on the available list. I'm getting a bit fed up of all this "me time" now,' I joked. 'It's about time I had another placement.'

In all seriousness, I knew what would heal me the most and help me to move on after Shazia. It was doing what I loved – fostering another child – and I couldn't wait to see who came through my door next.

Acknowledgements

Thank you to my children, Tess, Pete and Sam, who are such a big part of my fostering today. However, I had not met you when Shazia, Michael and Louisa came into my home. To my wide circle of fostering friends – you know who you are! Your support and your laughter are valued. To my friend Andrew B for your continued encouragement and care. Thanks also to Heather Bishop who spent many hours listening and enabled this story to be told, my literary agent Rowan Lawton and to Anna Valentine at Trapeze for giving me the opportunity to share these stories.

FGM

- Female genital mutilation (FGM), sometimes known as 'female circumcision' or 'female genital cutting', is illegal in the UK.
- It's also illegal to take abroad a British national or permanent resident for FGM, or to help someone trying to do this.
- You can get up to 14 years in prison for carrying out FGM or helping it to take place.
- A case of FGM is either discovered or treated at a medical appointment in England every hour, according to analysis of NHS statistics.
- An estimated 200 million women and girls worldwide are affected by FGM.
- The NHS attended to 9,000 FGM cases in England last year (2017).

Help and Support
- Contact the police if you or someone you know is in immediate danger of FGM.

- Contact the Foreign and Commonwealth Office if you know a British national who's already been taken abroad. Telephone: 020 7008 1500
From overseas: +44 (0)20 7008 1500
- Contact the NSPCC anonymously if you're worried that a girl or young woman is at risk or is a victim of FGM.

NSPCC FGM Helpline
Email: fgmhelp@nspcc.org.uk
Telephone: 0800 028 3550
From overseas: +44 (0)800 028 3550
You can get help and advice in the UK from:

- Foundation for Women's Health Research and Development (FORWARD) – www.forwarduk.org.uk
- Daughters of Eve – www.dofeve.org

A Note from Maggie

I really hope you enjoyed reading about Shazia and Michael's stories. I love sharing my experiences of fostering with you, and I also love hearing what you think about them. If you enjoyed this book, or any of my others, please think about leaving a review online. I know other readers really benefit from your thoughts, and I do too.

To be the first to hear about my new books, you can keep in touch on my Facebook page @MaggieHartleyAuthor. I find it inspiring to learn about your own experiences of fostering and adoption, and to read your comments and reviews.

Finally, thank you so much for choosing to read *Sold to be a Wife*. If you enjoyed it, there are others available including *Too Scared to Cry*, *Tiny Prisoners*, *The Little Ghost Girl*, *A Family for Christmas*, *Too Young to be a Mum*, *Who Will Love Me Now*, *The Girl No One Wanted*, *Battered, Broken, Healed*, and *Is It My Fault Mummy?*. I hope you'll enjoy my next story just as much.

Maggie Hartley

TINY PRISONERS

Evie and Elliot are scrawny, filthy and wide-eyed with fear when they turn up on foster carer Maggie Hartley's doorstep. They're too afraid to leave the house and any intrusion of the outside world sends them into a panic. It's up to Maggie to unlock the truth of their heartbreaking upbringing, and to help them learn to smile again.

THE LITTLE GHOST GIRL

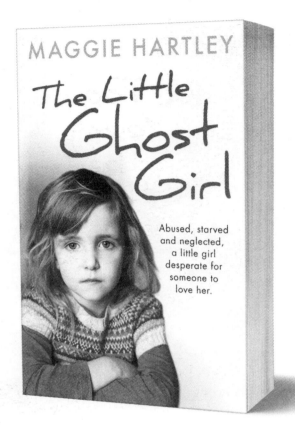

Ruth is a ghost of a girl when she arrives into foster mother Maggie Hartley's care. Pale, frail and withdrawn, it's clear to Maggie that Ruth had seen and experienced things that no 11-year-old should have to. Ruth is in desperate need of help, but can Maggie get through to her and unearth the harrowing secret she carries?

TOO YOUNG TO BE A MUM

When sixteen-year-old Jess arrives on foster carer Maggie Hartley's doorstep with her newborn son Jimmy, she has nowhere else to go. With social services threatening to take baby Jimmy into care, Jess knows that Maggie is her only chance of keeping her son. Can Maggie help Jess learn to become a mum?

WHO WILL LOVE ME NOW?

MAGGIE HARTLEY

Who Will Love Me Now?

Neglected, abused
and rejected.
A little girl desperate for
a home to call her own.

When ten-year-old Kirsty arrives at the home of foster carer
Maggie Hartley, she is reeling from the rejection of her
long-term foster family. She acts out, smashing up Maggie's
home. But when she threatens to hurt the baby boy Maggie
has fostered since birth, Maggie is placed in an impossible
position; one that calls into question her decision to
become a foster carer in the first place…

BATTERED, BROKEN, HEALED

Six-week-old baby Jasmine comes to stay with Maggie after she is removed from her home. Neighbours have repeatedly called the police on suspicion of domestic violence, but her timid mother Hailey vehemently denies that anything is wrong. Can Maggie persuade Hailey to admit what's going on behind closed doors so that mother and baby can be reunited?

DENIED A MUMMY

Maggie has her work cut out for her when her latest placement arrives on her doorstep; two little boys, aged five and seven and their eight-year-old sister. Having suffered extensive abuse and neglect, Maggie must slowly work through their trauma with love and care. But when a couple is approved to adopt the siblings, alarm bells start to ring. Maggie tries to put her own fears to one side but she can't shake the feeling of dread as she waves goodbye to them. Will these vulnerable children ever find a forever family?

TOO SCARED TO CRY

A baby too scared to cry. Two toddlers too scared to speak. This is the dramatic short story of three traumatised siblings, whose lives are transformed by the love of foster carer Maggie Hartley.

A FAMILY FOR CHRISTMAS

MAGGIE HARTLEY

A Family for Christmas

When a tragic accident scars a family, will it take a miracle to heal them?

SHORT STORY

A tragic accident leaves the life of toddler Edward
changed forever and his family wracked with guilt.
Will Maggie be able to help this family grieve for the son
they've lost and learn to love the little boy he is now?
And will Edward have a family to go home to
at Christmas?

THE GIRL NO ONE WANTED

Eleven-year-old Leanne is out of control. With over forty placements in her short life, no local foster carers are willing to take in this angry and damaged little girl. Maggie is Leanne's only hope, and her last chance. If this placement fails, Leanne will have to be put in a secure unit. Where most others would simply walk away, Maggie refuses to give up on the little girl who's never known love.

IS IT MY FAULT MUMMY?

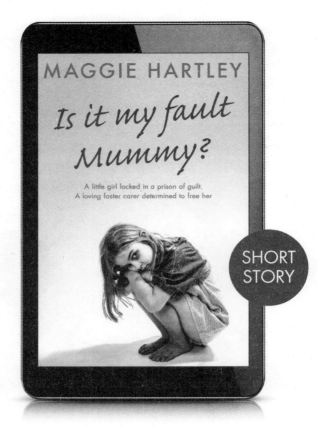

Seven-year-old Paris is trapped in a prison of guilt.
Devastated after the death of her baby brother, Joel,
Maggie faces one of the most heartbreaking cases yet as
she tries to break down the wall of guilt surrounding this
damaged little girl.